REACT
HARNESS YOUR ANIMAL BRAIN

Professor Robert West
Jamie West

Contents

About This Book

A few years ago, I had an idea to write a series of short, accessible guides to psychology based on the principles I was teaching in workshops and lectures around the world.

I wanted to include the kind of information that is invaluable in a practical sense but also fascinating to talk about.

I asked my son Jamie, a writer and musician, if he would be interested in writing the books with me. Shortly after we began talking through the project, he suggested that presenting conversations between us might be a fun way for readers to learn about the topics.

The writing process was simple: we'd go out to my local Italian restaurant, chat through a range of psychology principles culled from decades of research (mine and other people's), then he'd trim, edit and polish the conversations to make them vaguely comprehensible.

React: Harness Your Animal Brain is the second book in this series, a sequel to *Energise: The Secrets Of Motivation*. However, you can read the books in any order as we recap any relevant information you might need.

I hope that these conversations will help you to understand the nature of our 'animal brains' and how to harness that knowledge to achieve your goals. Enjoy!

Robert West

1. What Is Our Animal Brain?

Jamie Here we are again! Ready to solve the mysteries of psychology and end human suffering for good. This time, we're discussing the 'animal brain' and how to harness it to shape behaviour. So, Professor West, where do we begin?

Robert Glad to be back. Well, the first thing to say is that, for the purposes of this book, it's useful to think about our brains as being split into two parts: our 'human brain' and our 'animal brain'. This helps us to figure out what's driving behaviour, both our own and other people's. And being able to understand and explain behaviour can make it easier to *change* behaviour.

Jamie I know a little bit about how the brain works from things I've read over the years, but I still feel mostly in the dark.

Robert Learning about the animal brain lifts the lid on behaviour that, otherwise, seems very mysterious! There's a lot of fascinating research that will transform your understanding of human behaviour.

Jamie Big claims! I'll try to stay awake. So, what exactly is our animal brain?

Robert Let's start by agreeing that humans are, first and foremost, animals.

Jamie At school, the comeback taunt was always, 'You may be an animal but *I'm* not!'

Robert Yes, well ... we all certainly *are*. It's no insult! We evolved over many millions of years, and our existence as humans is very recent in the Earth's history. A lot of our brain is pretty similar to how it was before the 'human brain' – the self-conscious part capable of language – came on the scene.

Jamie So, when we say 'animal brain', we're referring to the part of our brain that evolved before humans emerged as a separate species. We're into theory-of-evolution territory, right?

Robert Yes. And this part of our brain has many commonalities with other animals like mice, pigeons, and, of course, apes. And there are many things in our brain that operate at that level.

Jamie But it's not as though you could just remove the human part of our brain and it would then be the same as the brain of an orangutan or a mouse?

Robert (*laughs*) No! The key point is that the animal part of our brain has a lot of similarities with the brains of other animals – to varying degrees, depending on the animal. And studying how a mouse responds to rewards, for example, can shed a surprising amount of light on our own behaviour. Similarly, understanding the process of training a dog can actually help us to more effectively 'train' ourselves, so to speak.

Jamie Well, I'm looking forward to that chapter! What would you say are the main features of the animal brain?

Robert When we talk about the animal brain, we'll be talking primarily about *instincts*, *habits* and *feelings*.

Jamie We looked at instincts in our first book, *Energise*, didn't we? I remember you saying that breathing was an example of an instinct – something we do without having to consciously think about it.

Robert Right. An instinct is an *innate stimulus-impulse association*.

Jamie And in English?

Robert The easiest way to understand it is through an example. So, when a mother herring gull sees something that looks like the open beak of a chick, it will regurgitate food into that beak. The stimulus is the open beak, and the associated impulse is to regurgitate the food. It's also sometimes called a 'fixed-action pattern'.

Jamie I see. So, similarly, we don't need to be taught to breathe as babies, that's innate. But we can decide to hold our breath – so, can we control our instincts?

Robert Up to a point. The bird obviously couldn't 'decide' not to feed its chick just for the sake of it. But as humans, we can hold our breath and override other instincts – like not blinking during a staring contest.

Jamie All right. Next up on your list are habits. I'm pretty sure I know what a habit is – brushing teeth, eating breakfast every morning etc.

Robert Correct. But habits also include fairly simple things that we might not think to consider, such as walking. We spent a lot of time as toddlers learning how to balance and walk, but now we rarely have to think about the mechanics of putting one foot in front of the other.

Jamie Our lives are filled with habits, not just the usual ones we tend to think of.

Robert Precisely. And finally, we also experience feelings. Things like anger, anxiety, happiness or sadness – to name a few.

Jamie That's what those are? *Feelings?*

Robert Yes – it seems obvious, but stick with me. We also feel hunger and thirst which come from *drive states*, and I'll talk more about these later. In addition, we respond to sensory experiences, which can be pleasurable or painful. And, crucially, we have feelings of *want* and *need* that lie at the heart of motivation.

Jamie So, when we think about the animal brain, we mean instincts, habits, and feelings. And feelings include emotional states, drives, sensory experiences, and wants and needs. We really share all of this with other animals?

Robert Pretty much.

Jamie That's quite a lot going on there.

Robert Absolutely! The animal brain is complex, and it's highly evolved to ensure that we survive and pass on our DNA. And going back to your playground insults, it's important to note that if we deny the animal part of our nature, we're not going to get very far in understanding or working with ourselves.

Jamie What would you say is the main difference between the 'animal brain' and the 'human brain'?

Robert The human brain is an equally big subject and we'll be looking at it in detail in our next book in the series, *Reflect: The Science Of Decision Making*. But, for now, I'd say the main difference is that the human brain is self-conscious. This means we can reflect on our behaviour and experiences.

THE ANIMAL BRAIN IS VERY COMPLEX, YOU KNOW

Jamie We can tell each other what we're thinking and feeling.

Robert Or our best *guess* at what we're thinking and feeling.

Jamie Our best guess?

Robert Let's say it's January 1st and my New Year's resolution is to eat healthier. I find myself in a restaurant, and I see a Fiorentina pizza on the menu.

Jamie My favourite.

Robert My animal brain feels anticipated pleasure at the thought of the Fiorentina. My human brain communicates my want to the waiter, and they bring me my pizza. It sounds pretty simple, but, before I placed my order, there's a good chance the human part of my brain was reflecting on whether it would be a good decision or not. Should I really be eating pizza now? Could I pick a healthier choice?

Jamie Fiorentina does have spinach on it ... But I take your point – the animal part of your brain wants you to eat, but your human brain can take a moment to reflect on whether it's actually something you truly want.

Robert Exactly. And we often misinterpret our feelings. Sometimes the pizza might arrive and we realise we weren't as hungry as we thought.

Jamie That happens to me! I find it really hard to tell how hungry I am. My girlfriend always laughs at me because I order loads of food and then, after a few mouthfuls, I realise I'm going to need a doggy bag to take the rest home.

Robert Ah, but this is important. One of the things we can do to improve our satisfaction and enjoyment of life is to think carefully and genuinely about what we actually want. And it can be challenging to introspect accurately, and sometimes we'll make mistakes. But we also have to be careful we don't just go along with the narratives our society tells us about what we *should* want.

Jamie Society told you to order a Fiorentina pizza?

Robert Perhaps not in that particular example! But our experience of wanting and needing *can* be heavily influenced by stories told to us through our environment – advertisers, social media etc. Later in the book, we'll have a look at where wants and needs come from.

Jamie It sounds like the relationship between our human and animal brain is potentially very fraught. Stephen Fry said the great thing about a tree frog is that it doesn't wake up in the morning feeling guilty about being a bad tree frog the night before! Self-consciousness can feel like a bit of a curse sometimes.

Robert It's true. And a lot of the challenge of being a human is how we manage the interaction between the human and animal brain, which is a major theme of this book. When we talk about harnessing the animal brain, we're trying to figure out how our self-conscious, forward-thinking human brain can be used to better guide our animal brain.

Jamie So, even though we're talking about harnessing the animal brain, we're actually always dealing with both?

Robert That's right.

Jamie Okay! What else do we have in store for our readers?

Robert Plenty. We'll be learning why it's so easy to fall into unhealthy and even addictive behaviours. I'll explain how to overcome bad behaviour patterns and develop good habits. We'll take a deeper dive into our basic conditioning and look at the building blocks of behaviour. We'll discuss how the fundamental features of the animal brain play out in our professional and personal worlds, and how we can use them to our advantage. And, crucially, we'll look at how we can enable our animal brains to 'react' more effectively in our day-to-day lives.

Jamie Sounds good – I'm buckled up and ready to go!

KEY POINTS

- It is useful to think of the brain as being split into two parts: the *human brain* and the *animal brain*. The human brain is self-conscious, the animal brain is not.

- Both parts of the brain work together to get us to do things and not do things.

- Our animal brain evolved before the human species evolved. It still has many commonalities with the brains of other animals.

- The animal brain is complex and highly evolved to ensure that we survive and pass on our DNA.

- Understanding the animal brain helps us to explain behaviour, which makes it easier to change behaviour.

- The animal brain underpins our *instincts*, *habits* and *feelings*.

- It can be difficult to interpret our own emotions and feelings – for example, ordering a big meal then realising we're not as hungry as we thought.

- For humans, the experience of wanting and needing can be heavily influenced by narratives told to us by others.

2. Training The Animal Brain

Jamie We can train certain animals, to a greater or lesser extent. Can we train our own animal brains?

Robert Good question. Looking at how we train other animals is actually quite informative. Let's imagine I've got a dog, and I want to train it to bring me my newspaper in the morning.

Jamie I don't think Fitbit would approve.

Robert I'll take the dog for a walk later as a thank you! Anyway, like all good animal trainers, I would use something called *operant conditioning.*

Jamie I love jargon.

Robert Don't be put off by the name. Operant conditioning is a way the brain learns from reward and punishment. It means that the animal brain is learning an association between a particular behaviour in a particular situation and a reward or punishment.

Jamie So, giving your dog a Scooby Snack after he's done something good?

Robert Correct. The biscuit is the reward. And food for a hungry animal is what's known as a *primary reinforcer.*

Jamie Which is?

Robert Essentially, it's a stimulus that the animal brain is innately attracted to. For animals, it's often food and drink. And humans are the same, too. Have you ever wondered why event organisers offer free refreshments?

Jamie Because we like free stuff?

Robert Well, yes. But the refreshments are primary reinforcers. And just as the dog likes us for feeding it, we also tend to like people who feed us.

Jamie (*laughs*) I've never thought about it like that. So, these event organisers are actually tapping into something quite deep in our animal brains.

Robert It works pretty well – as long as the food isn't terrible.

Jamie Okay, let's get back to training your dog. Where do we start?

Robert So, we're trying to create a behaviour that didn't exist before, which is the dog fetching the newspaper.

Jamie And we're going to be using a primary reinforcer – a dog treat – to help it learn.

Robert Yes. We're also going to use a process called *successive approximation*.

Jamie These are coming thick and fast.

Robert It's a complicated name for a fairly simple thing. Successive approximation, essentially, is rewarding the animal brain in stages. So, at first, if the dog goes near the newspaper, you give it a treat. Then when the dog snuffles up to the paper, you give it another treat.

Jamie That's a lot of treats. What if your dog is on a diet?

Robert You can make sure the treat is small. But here's the next important point: once it's snuffled up to the newspaper, you no longer reward it for just going *near* the newspaper. You only reward it for the most recent stage. Otherwise, it won't learn to progress.

Jamie That's very clever. Then what?

Robert You offer the newspaper to the dog, giving it the opportunity to put it in its mouth. Then you reward it with a treat.

Jamie What if I want to teach the dog to pick up the newspaper when it's posted through the letterbox?

Robert Ah, that would be ideal! But how would the dog know that the newspaper was there?

Jamie Uh...

Robert It would hear it drop through the letterbox. So, you want to train your dog to move close to the door when the letterbox rattles. And to train that behaviour, you would go to the letterbox, create the sound, and reward the dog for coming close. You get the idea.

Jamie So, you can train quite complicated behaviours by rewarding them bit by bit.

Robert That's how they get dogs running up ramps and jumping through hoops.

Jamie What happens when the behaviour has been learned? Do you need to keep giving the dog treats?

Robert Once you've established the desired behaviour, you don't need to reward the dog with a biscuit every time. You can give it a social reward instead, like saying 'well done' and giving it a pat on the head.

Jamie Ah, like you might say 'well done' to a child?

Robert Pretty much. Both dogs and humans are social creatures and, therefore, sensitive to social rewards.

Jamie You make it sound quite logical and easy, but I think it would probably take quite a long time to train a dog.

Robert It does require patience, and some dogs are more trainable than others. But there are extra tricks you can use. Have you seen anyone use a clicker with their dog?

Jamie What's that?

Robert A clicker is a small gadget that literally makes a clicking noise. Trainers use it all the time.

Jamie   Now you mention it, I have seen those. What do they do?

Robert   The noise a clicker makes is what we call a *secondary reinforcer.* As soon as the dog performs the behaviour you want, you press the clicker, then give the dog a treat. The click signals that food is coming, and this adds an extra motivation for the dog.

Jamie   Wouldn't it be faster to give the animal food without wasting time with the click?

Robert   It's a crucial signal to the brain that a primary reinforcer, i.e. the food, will be coming soon – even if it's only going to be in a second or two. It helps the brain make an *immediate* connection between the desired behaviour and the reward.

Jamie   Now I think about it, the mouse on my computer clicks when I press it . . .

Robert   Well observed! In that context, the click lets you know that some small reward, such as a browser opening, is about to happen. Another example would be a loading icon spinning round.

Jamie   But I wouldn't have said the clicks and icons were rewarding in themselves, though.

Robert   You're right. That's why they're *secondary* reinforcers. But, interestingly, they can prompt you to perform a particular behaviour. For example, the sound your phone makes when you get a notification. It lets you know something has happened, so you pick up your phone to see what it is. But the notification sound itself isn't intrinsically rewarding.

Jamie It's often just an annoying app sending you a 'push notification'.

Robert And what do you do then?

Jamie I turn off notifications for the app!

Robert Because it's not giving you a reward. In fact, it probably feels like a punishment: 'I wasted my time checking my phone for this?!'

Jamie And then there's the little flag telling me a new email has come in, so I open it up, but, again, it's usually spam or something I don't care about.

Robert Right. And we're going to talk about this later – how technology trains and controls our animal brains without actually making us feel good.

Jamie All this talk of training reminds me of an article in *The New York Times* about a woman who tried to train her husband using techniques she learned from exotic animal trainers.

Robert That sounds . . . interesting!

Jamie She was trying to get him to stop leaving dirty shirts on the floor and that sort of thing. So, she'd thank him every time he put his shirts in the laundry basket. And instead of telling her husband off when he forgot his keys, she'd offer no response at all.

Robert Sticking with the praise and avoiding punishment. How did it work out in the end?

Jamie Apparently, she was quite successful. Although after she told her husband what she was up to, he started using the same techniques on her!

Robert As I said, these techniques can sometimes work on humans. But humans have the ability to notice and reflect, so you may need to be more subtle about it. I wouldn't advocate using a clicker on your partner!

Jamie Good advice . . . Now, I feel like we've just explored a huge amount of information. So, let me see if I've got this right. If I want to train my dog, I'm going to do this through *operant conditioning*, which means teaching it through reward and punishment.

Robert Correct.

Jamie I will also use *successive approximation*, which means that I'm going to reward it in stages. As it progresses towards the behaviour I want, I'm only going to reward it for the most recent stage.

Robert You've got it.

Jamie And I'm going to use a *primary reinforcer* to reward it. For animals, this is often food and drink, but it could be something else like praise or a pat on the head.

Robert Keep going.

Jamie I can also use a *secondary reinforcer* – like a clicker – immediately after the dog has performed the behaviour to signal to it that the reward is on its way.

Robert Give the boy a biscuit!

Jamie Thank you.

Robert While you're munching on that, I can say that the animal brain in humans often responds quite similarly to the animal brain in animals! Obviously, things aren't always as straightforward as that. But these basics are helpful in understanding what drives human motivation.

Jamie I'll be honest, I don't often go around thinking about reward and punishment when I want things from other people.

Robert Perhaps not consciously. But if you want to influence other people's behaviour, and even your own, understanding the nature of rewards and the timing of those rewards is crucial. Luckily, that's exactly what we're going to talk about next.

KEY POINTS

- The animal brain learns from reward and punishment through a process called *operant conditioning*.

- In operant conditioning, the animal brain creates an association between the behaviour, the situation, and the reward or punishment – for example, giving a dog a biscuit for following instructions.

- With operant conditioning, you should aim to deliver the reward as soon after the behaviour you're trying to encourage as possible.

- A *primary reinforcer* is a stimulus that the animal brain is innately attracted to, such as food or drink.

- A *secondary reinforcer* is a stimulus that the animal brain learns to associate with a primary reinforcer – for example, a dog-clicker indicating food is coming soon.

- Secondary reinforcers nudge you to perform particular behaviours – for example, a notification sound will trigger you to pick up your phone.

- *Successive approximation* involves training an animal's behaviour in stages, only rewarding the most recent stage.

3. Timings Of Rewards

Jamie Let's delve a little deeper into how our brain gets rewarded. You said in the last chapter that the timing of the reward matters.

Robert Yes. In general, it's important to reward the behaviour you're trying to encourage immediately – like with the dog-clicker. But scientists have also studied what happens when you don't reward behaviour every single time, and it makes for pretty interesting reading.

Jamie Go on.

Robert Let's imagine a rat, a cage, and a lever –

Jamie This sounds like the start of a bad joke.

Robert Bear with me. The general idea is: when the rat presses the lever, food is dispensed. But, in this experiment, the rat doesn't get food *every* time the lever is pressed. Instead, it only gets food after it's pressed the lever 20 times.

Jamie So, for the first 19 presses there's nothing, but on the 20th, it's dinner time.

Robert Correct.

Jamie Why would the rat press the lever in the first place?

Robert It might press it accidentally or out of curiosity. The first time it does it, we would release food so that it makes the connection between the lever and food. But after that, we'll only give it food if it presses the lever 20 times. So, how do you think the rat will behave in this scenario?

Jamie I guess it would press the lever as fast as it could 20 times.

Robert Ah – that's because you're human, and I've told you how the experiment works. In fact, the rat will start to press the lever fairly slowly at first. Then, when the food arrives, it will begin to figure out that it has to press the lever many times to get food. So, it will start off pressing the lever slowly again, and then, as it gets closer to the food, it will speed up pressing the lever.

Jamie Curious.

Robert What we're doing in this experiment is using a *fixed-ratio schedule of reinforcement*.

Jamie Another one for the vocab diary?

Robert Indeed. I know the jargon can be a little intimidating, but it's useful to know. Essentially, a fixed-ratio schedule of reinforcement just means that the rewards are given after a fixed number of responses – in this case, 20.

Jamie Right. But why would the rat even be bothered to press the lever 20 times?

Robert Good question. If we raised the number of times the rat needs to press the lever before it gets food from 20 to 30, do you think it would keep going?

Jamie Putting myself in the mind of a rat, I'm going to say no because the rewards are too far apart.

Robert You're correct. It does depend on the exact set-up of the experiment, but if you put the number up too high, it will lead to *ratio-strain*, which will lead to the rat giving up.

Jamie I think writing a book can feel that way sometimes – all the reward of publication and acclaim is just too far away! I find I have to set mini-goals along the way.

Robert Absolutely. You have to reward the behaviour you want to encourage as you go along, or signal that a reward is on its way with secondary reinforcers.

Jamie I break it down into smaller chunks, like setting an aim to finish a chapter, half a chapter, or even just a paragraph. That way I can feel good when I reach a mini-milestone. And at the end of every writing session, I email myself words of encouragement – things like: 'Jamie, you rock!' It's a surprisingly feel-good moment!

Robert (*laughs*) It's a great idea. Even though it might feel silly to do, the research tells us that this kind of self-reward can actually work.

Jamie Back to the rats. What do the mad scientists do next?

Robert They put in secondary reinforcers. In this case, it's a light that flashes every fifth time the rat presses the lever. And this keeps the rat on track to get the food after 30 presses.

Jamie Wow. The rat associates the light with the food, and even though the light itself isn't rewarding, and it doesn't flash every time, it lets the rat know food is coming – so it motivates it to keep pressing the lever.

Robert It's pretty clever, right?

Jamie It actually makes me think of video games. If you're navigating a landscape and trying to find the right way to go, the designers often light up the correct path so that you can follow it.

Robert That's a good example. The lesson there is: if you want to encourage behaviours that have rewards quite far apart, you can use secondary reinforcers to keep people motivated.

Jamie Adventure games also sometimes give a musical cue if you're close to solving a puzzle, but you're not quite there yet.

Robert Perfect. Evidently, the game designers are incorporating rewards that target the animal brain.

Jamie But what happens if the reward isn't given after a fixed number of responses? What if it's more random?

Robert Very good question. Do you remember we talked about checking notifications on our phones?

Jamie Do I remember ten minutes ago? Yes.

Robert (*laughs*) Okay, well! Think again about the notifications you get. How many times are you being notified of something you actually want to know about?

Jamie Like I said, I've switched off a lot of notifications, but I still get plenty of useless ones.

Robert How do you know they're useless?

Jamie Because I check my phone . . .

Robert So, you can't tell by the notification sound whether or not you have an interesting message. The sound is a signal – it may give a sense of anticipation, but you have to check your phone to find out what the notification is pointing to.

Jamie And even though it might be something important, it's usually stupidly trivial.

Robert I'm sensing anger, Jamie. On average, maybe one out of every five notifications is interesting, but, despite this, you'll keep checking your phone anyway.

Jamie I need to learn how to control myself!

Robert Easier said than done. This is deep animal psychology, and the people who design phones and social media know how to exploit our biological reward systems. It hits our animal brain in a way our human brain struggles to control. For the nerds, like me, the timing of this intermittent reward is called a *variable-ratio schedule of reinforcement.*

Jamie Because the rewards come after a variable number of responses, I see. How does that schedule work on our hypothetical rats?

Robert It means they press the lever pretty much constantly. Rewarding the animal brain after varying numbers of responses is incredibly powerful.

Jamie It sounds a bit like playing golf. Even though I mostly hit terrible shots, every once in a while I'll hit a great shot, and it feels so wonderful!

Robert And golf is quite an extreme version because when you hit a bad shot, it's pretty punishing.

Jamie All kinds of examples are springing to mind now ... Is this why nagging can become such an ingrained habit? If you nag your partner to tidy up and they never do, eventually you will give up and stop nagging. But if they respond to it occasionally, you might end up thinking that your nagging has worked, so you keep on doing it?

Robert That's it – variable-ratio schedule of reinforcement.

Jamie Which must also be behind the power of gambling – it only rewards people occasionally, and they never know when the reward will come.

Robert And it is hugely, hugely addictive for a lot of people.

Jamie I'm guessing we should be wary of these activities that only reward us intermittently and unpredictably?

Robert They're not all bad. A lot of people get a huge amount of enjoyment from golf, for example. But you're right. We need to be very careful, especially with things like gambling and social media.

Jamie So, we've seen what happens when we reward behaviour after a fixed number of responses and after a variable number of responses – what else is there?

Robert Another interesting variation is where the rat has to respond *infrequently* to get the reward. If it responds too often, the reward doesn't come.

Jamie I don't follow. If the rat presses the lever too often, it doesn't get the food?

Robert There are activities we do where we need to learn to go slowly and control ourselves. We can't rush them. Things like running a marathon. You can't physically sprint the distance –

Jamie You've clearly never seen Kipchoge run.

Robert But he's still pacing himself. He just runs a lot faster than you do! And there will be lots of little rewards along the way, letting him know he's on the right track. Signs saying, '15 miles to go', 'Ten miles to go' etc.

Jamie I once tried an app on my phone that was supposed to calm me down and teach me to be more patient. You had to slowly move your finger across the screen, and if you moved it too fast, you had to start again.

Robert How did that go?

Jamie I hated it! I got really frustrated, and I came away feeling angry. So, it did the opposite of its job. Although, maybe that was just me.

Robert Slowing down our response can be difficult for humans. How many people attempt to put flat pack furniture together without reading the instructions?

Jamie You saw my IKEA desk, huh?

Robert It was supposed to be a desk? Anyway, my point is that you're not alone. This is *impulse control*. The human brain can try to read the instructions, but the animal brain just gets fed up.

Jamie So, I should probably keep going with the patience training, then? I'll need to re-download the app ...

Robert That app probably isn't for you. But even just having an understanding of what's going on inside your brain can help you figure out strategies that may be more successful. For example, saying to yourself, 'This is one of the times when I naturally want to rush, but I actually need to take a breath and slow down.'

Jamie Recognising there's a part of me that wants to speed ahead allows me to create some distance from that feeling.

Robert Exactly – although, of course, there will be times when you may need to use a different tactic. That said, at least you'll have managed to frame the problem in a useful way.

Jamie I've heard you talk about these schedules of reinforcement in the past and found it a bit hard to understand – but now I see that, given how powerful rewards and punishments are, the timing of them is also crucial. And even though, as humans, we can all feel very complicated and clever, sometimes we just respond in the same way as our poor rat in its cage.

Robert Knowing about these different schedules helps us understand how our environment is shaping our behaviour, often without us realising it. This allows us to recalibrate our environment, and how we deliver rewards, to better suit our needs.

Jamie The variable-ratio-schedule of reinforcement sounds particularly powerful.

Robert It is. And it can keep you doing activities that have a very negative impact on your life.

Jamie The more we talk about that one in particular, the more examples I can think of. How about the 'friend' who is occasionally kind and charming but is quite distant or demanding the rest of the time? That variable reward can keep people locked in relationships that are actually quite bad for them.

Robert Of course, in the real-world there are always multiple factors at play. But it's definitely something to watch out for.

Jamie Good idea. We'd better move on before I get side-tracked thinking of more examples!

KEY POINTS

- The timing of rewards is extremely important to the animal brain.

- A *fixed-ratio schedule of reinforcement* is when rewards are delivered after a fixed number of responses – for example, a rat is given food every 20 times it presses a lever.

- If the number of responses needed for the reward becomes too large, it causes *ratio-strain,* and the animal brain gives up.

- To motivate behaviours in which a lot of responses are needed for the main goal to be achieved, *secondary reinforcers* can be used – for example, game designers play musical cues as the player gets closer to solving a puzzle.

- A *variable-ratio schedule of reinforcement* is when rewards are delivered after varying numbers of responses – for example, gambling on a slot machine. This schedule affects your animal brain in a way your human brain struggles to control.

- Understanding the different schedules helps us to see how our environment is shaping our behaviour, often without our awareness. This knowledge allows us to recalibrate our environment and change how we deliver rewards to better suit our needs.

4. Wants And Needs

Jamie Let's take a closer look at *wants* and *needs*. I've heard you talk about how important they are, but – to be honest – I don't really know much more than that.

Robert Wants and needs are at the absolute heart of understanding the animal brain. Quite simply, wants and needs get us to do things. Some of these things are obvious, like eating, drinking and procreating. But there's also a great many other things that help us function.

Jamie So, without wants and needs, we're not going to be motivated to do much of anything. But what exactly is a 'want'?

Robert A 'want' is a feeling of anticipated pleasure linked to some imagined scenario.

Jamie Like, right now, I want the last slice of garlic bread?

Robert Exactly. But, let me ask you this – do you feel like you need it?

Jamie Hmm... I wouldn't say I *need* it.

Robert Why not?

Jamie Because we only just had lunch.

Robert Ha! Okay, now imagine that you've been locked up in a dungeon for a week without any food.

Jamie That took a dark turn!

Robert If I came into the room and put that slice of garlic bread on the floor, would you need it then?

Jamie Yes!

Robert Why?

Jamie Because I'd be starving.

Robert And the garlic bread would relieve that discomfort?

Jamie Right. Although, I'm not sure I want to play out this scenario anymore.

Robert It's just an illustration to show that a 'need' is a feeling of anticipated relief from discomfort of some kind.

Jamie So, when I need something, it's to get rid of a bad feeling – like being really hungry. And when I want something, it's because I expect it to make me feel good.

Robert Exactly. In everyday life, we often use the terms 'want' and 'need' interchangeably, but it's useful to employ these more precise psychological definitions because they help us to understand behaviour more clearly.

Jamie I'm taking this garlic bread before you ask any more questions about it ... Presumably, you can want and need something at the same time?

Robert Yes. If you were even just a bit hungry, you could both want and need to eat that slice of garlic bread. You'd be looking forward to the pleasure of eating it and the relief from the discomfort of hunger.

Jamie Can you need something that you don't want?

Robert That can happen, especially in addiction, which we'll look at in more detail later. But as a quick example: someone can need nicotine – the active drug in cigarettes – without actually wanting it. Now, let me ask you a question: what sorts of things do you think you need?

Jamie Lots of things! Food, water, oxygen, the England cricket team to win the Ashes!

Robert I can't help you with that last one, but let's look at the first two on your list – food and water – because they bring us onto the idea of *drives*. Drive states basically get us to do things irrespective of our 'want' to do them. So, with hunger, your body requires nutrition, and the drive creates a tension inside of you to make sure you eat.

Jamie And that tension is obviously a feeling of hunger. I presume thirst works the same way?

Robert Yes. Drives are our body's way of keeping its functions working. You need oxygen, water and food in order to live. These drive states are essential because if we needed to remember to breathe or eat or drink every single time, we wouldn't last very long.

Jamie I forget to eat lunch quite often if I'm busy.

Robert And what happens?

Jamie I get hangry.

Robert (*laughs*) Missing a meal is not necessarily a big deal, but you'd definitely feel it after 24 hours without food.

Jamie I don't even want to find out. In fact, I'm very driven *not* to find out! Am I using that correctly?

Robert Not really. In regular conversation, we often use the word 'driven' to describe a person who's powerfully motivated to achieve certain goals – money, status, success etc. Here, we're using the word 'drive' in a different and specific way.

Jamie Point taken. So, how do these specific drives work?

Robert The drives I'm talking about – things like hunger, thirst and breathing – follow a *homeostatic process*. Your body needs to do particular behaviours at certain times in order to keep it functioning – like eating and drinking at regular intervals. Your body has lots of brain circuits that act like thermostats to keep the concentrations of chemicals within acceptable limits to keep you alive. These circuits send signals to the part of your brain that creates the experience of needing things. This feels like a kind of tension or a sense of discomfort.

Jamie Drive states create an uncomfortable feeling – like being thirsty when we haven't drunk enough. You're saying drives create needs?

Robert That's right.

Jamie But it all seems very 'feeling' based to me. I mean, how can we measure wants and needs? If we're looking at an animal, how can we tell if it wants something? We can't exactly ask it?

Robert Essentially, you have to make a diagnosis on the basis of the outcome. So if you see your cat clawing at the food cupboard, you'll likely guess that it's hungry. It's the same with humans –

Jamie If you see me clawing at the food cupboard . . .

Robert (*laughs*) Right.

Jamie But surely, as humans, we can just tell each other what we want?

Robert As I mentioned earlier, it can actually be surprisingly hard for us to introspect and find out what we really want or need. We need to learn how to do it. A child wriggling in their chair might not realise that they need to go to the toilet.

Jamie When I was kid, I remember occasions when I was quite adamant that I didn't need to go to the loo when, rather embarrassingly, it turned out that I did.

Robert And you hardly ever make that mistake anymore!

Jamie Hilarious.

Robert The point is, it does take some learning to understand the signals our body is sending. And even as adults, especially as one gets older, the need to go to the toilet can come on more suddenly and urgently.

Jamie But we must get better at decoding the signals our body is sending over time. How good are we at measuring our own wants and needs?

Robert Psychologists often ask people to rate their wants and needs on a scale. And it turns out that asking people to quantify their feelings can be extremely useful in understanding and predicting their behaviour. Of course, it's subject to quite a lot of potential bias and error because it's hard to introspect accurately. But there are ways to counter that problem.

Jamie Can you give me an example of quantifying our wants and needs?

Robert Here's a simple one: if you show a child several toys then ask them which one they like the most, their answer will predict which toy they'll actually choose to take home. It seems pretty obvious, but the important point here is that you can quantify subjective experiences. And once you've got those feelings in numerical form, you've got data you can work with and use to draw possible conclusions.

Jamie I think I often struggle to know what I really want.

Robert That's common in modern society because a lot of basic needs are taken care of. Most people are not worrying about where their next meal is coming from. So that means we're spending a lot of our life operating on more marginal wants and needs – things we don't necessarily feel that strongly about. And advertisers work on this principle a lot, showing us enticing pictures of shiny phones and stylish clothes.

Jamie But we *do* feel strongly about them!

Robert We often feel strongly about them *after* they're advertised to us.

Jamie Maybe you're right. The other day, I followed a link advertising a hotel to me. The images were very appealing, and I felt like I wanted to stay there. But the more I looked through the website, the more I felt a kind of need as well. And then a message popped up on the site, saying that five other people were looking at the same room *right now.* My desire suddenly became urgent – not very rational, not very 'human brain'.

Robert It sounds as though they created an anxiety in you which super-charged your want – they created a sense that you were going to miss out to these 'other people' viewing the site! But you also said that the images were appealing.

Jamie Yes! Beautiful large rooms, a balcony, a bath...

Robert Wants and needs respond strongly to images, the more vivid the better.

Jamie It sounds very manipulative to me.

Robert In a way. Although, if the hotel really is as nice as promised, and you do actually want to go on a holiday, then perhaps it's not so bad. Of course, this moves us into the world of ethics, and that's a conversation for another day.

Jamie I suppose emotive images and adverts can be put to good use as well. I've seen some imaginative adverts discouraging people from drink-driving. There was one where a bartender asks a guy what he wants to drink, then the lighting changes, and suddenly the bartender puts on the voice of a police officer, then a judge in the courtroom. It was a very clever way to make the consequences feel real.

Robert I remember that one – it elicited powerful emotions in a way that just giving the statistics for road deaths doesn't.

Jamie It sounds as though when it comes to the animal brain, we can't just reel off a list of facts and figures and expect it to respond. We need to activate imaginations to engage emotions.

Robert And images can be very powerful even when you just conjure them with words. Think about listening to the radio or a podcast – the language used appeals to the senses and conjures an experience. People talk about the importance of 'painting a picture' or 'setting the scene' when we're storytelling.

Jamie I always felt Henry Blofeld, the cricket commentator, did that exceptionally well on *Test Match Special*. He'd talk you through the view from the commentary box, the number of pigeons pecking about, trivial things that – under his gaze – became interesting! But it can't be all emotion, can it? Facts and figures are there for a reason.

Robert Absolutely. And facts and figures *can* be used to create emotion in us – fear, for example. But, generally, they speak more to the rational human part of our brain. The main takeaway is that our animal brain underpins our experience of the world. So if we want to change behaviours, we absolutely cannot discount it.

Jamie I see. But beyond the homeostatic process, where do these wants and needs actually come from?

Robert I'm glad you asked – that's exactly what I want to talk about next . . .

KEY POINTS

- A *want* is a feeling of anticipated pleasure linked to an imagined scenario.

- A *need* is a feeling of anticipated relief from discomfort.

- Our bodies have *drives*, like hunger and thirst, that keep them functioning.

- Drives follow a *homeostatic process* which keeps us internally balanced – for example, if we haven't eaten in a while, our body creates an uncomfortable feeling of hunger.

- Asking people to quantify their own wants and needs can be very useful, even though the information will inevitably contain bias and errors.

- Wants and needs are strongly affected by vivid images that engage our emotions. They are less affected by lists of facts and figures.

5. Sources Of Wants And Needs

Jamie Before we continue, I just want to make sure I've got this right: we 'want' things because we think they're going to make us feel good, and we 'need' things because we think they'll stop us feeling bad?

Robert You've got it. Even though wants and needs are subjective, there are many that are common to all of us. Broadly speaking, they can be split into three categories: *biological, psychological* and *social*. Which one do you fancy taking on first?

Jamie Choice! Let's do *biological wants and needs*.

Robert Okay, so we've spoken about some of these already. Things like oxygen, thirst, hunger and tiredness are all feelings that are directly linked to basic life functions.

Jamie And they follow a *homeostatic process* which means they're regulated by the body which sends your brain signals when you 'need' something. And you experience this as tension or discomfort.

Robert Very good! Then there are biological wants and needs that relate to reproduction: sexual gratification, familial affection and nurturing.

Jamie Feelings that get us to make babies and then bring them up.

Robert Correct. Can you think of any others?

Jamie I'm wondering about defence and protection, things to do with responding to threats.

Robert Yes, these are wants and needs that deal with our safety and the safety of the people and things we care about. These are linked to feelings like pain, anger and fear.

Jamie And they trigger the fight or flight response?

Robert Indeed.

Biological Sources Of Wants And Needs

Respiration: Taking oxygen into the body and removing carbon dioxide.

Hydration: Maintaining adequate fluid balance.

Nutrition: Taking in nutrients.

Waste elimination: Removing solid and liquid waste.

Safety: Avoiding or escaping danger.

Rest: Recovering from exertion.

Sleep: Mental and physical recuperation.

Reproduction: Creating the next generation.

Jamie Let's move onto *psychological wants and needs.*

Robert These include pleasant sensations – for example, lying down on clean, freshly ironed linen or looking at beautiful scenery –

Jamie Or eating mutter paneer! Or the smell of a freshly baked baguette, or a lawn that's just been mowed, or –

Robert I see you've got the point.

Jamie I suppose the opposite is true, too? Our psychological wants and needs are to do with unpleasant sensations: loud, jarring noises or unattractive buildings.

Robert Yes, all of that. When you start to think about it, you can see how important the sensations of touch, taste, smell, sight and sound are to us. Which takes us into a very important source of wants and needs: aesthetics.

Jamie Fashion, design, art, music, architecture.

Robert Yes. Looking around, you can see how crucial it is for us humans to have things that please our senses.

Jamie People sometimes say that you don't need nice things in order to be content. But I do find I'm much happier in pleasant surroundings.

Robert Creative people tend to have a heightened aesthetic sense, so you may find it matters even more for you. But from a psychological perspective, we don't just need to have pleasant sensations, we also need to be stimulated. There is a lot of research that shows that infants need stimulation in order to develop and that carries over into our adult lives too. We need things to be going on around us, piquing our interest.

Jamie I once had a job in a library, and I'd often shelve books all day long. It literally felt like time had stopped.

Robert The boredom of youth – I think every generation has their version of it. I used to complain to my mother about being bored all the time and she would, without fail, tell me to go outside, get some fresh air and ride my bike.

Jamie There's an episode of *The Simpsons* where Homer tells Marge he's bored. And she says, 'Why don't you read something?' and he replies: 'Because I'm trying to *reduce* my boredom!'

Robert (*laughs*) Of course, having a sense of humour is important in life. We do have a desire to laugh and make jokes.

Jamie Since I started performing stand-up, I've become fascinated with comedy. It serves so many purposes: providing pleasure, helping us to cope, displaying human incompetence in amusing ways, I could go on! Anyway, what other psychological wants and needs are there?

Robert There are feelings linked to our sense of self: agency, self-respect, fulfilment and purpose.

Jamie Agency stands out to me as being incredibly important. I think we need to feel that we can have an impact on the world around us and at least some control over our destinies.

Robert Yes, it can be fundamental to our sense of wellbeing. And agency also includes our sense of being able to do and say what we want – in short, our sense of freedom. Without these, a part of us can wither away.

Jamie I'd say purpose is crucial as well.

Robert Absolutely. Feelings of fulfilment and purpose often go together. It might come from some kind of spirituality, or from a sense of being part of a bigger picture when it comes to humanity or the planet we live on. The key is that there is something outside of our own individual existence that gives meaning to our lives.

Jamie The thing is, even though none of this is new, it makes me realise that we don't often spend much time thinking about these elements separately or asking the question: what makes our lives meaningful to us?

Robert It can be very difficult to understand what our wants and needs are. And it can also be tempting to gloss over them because we just don't know what to do with them.

Jamie And I imagine if we're not great at understanding our own needs, we run the risk of dismissing other people's wants and needs too?

Robert Very much so.

Jamie It sounds as though there is overlap between our biological, psychological and social wants and needs.

Robert Yes. The three categories are not totally separate, but it's useful to classify them in this way so we can talk through them.

Psychological Sources Of Wants And Needs

To avoid physical discomfort: Not to feel pain or unpleasant physical sensations.

To avoid mental discomfort: Not to feel unpleasant mental states, such as anxiety, depression, frustration and cognitive dissonance (beliefs that conflict with each other).

To feel pleasant sensations: To experience enjoyable feelings which might be tactile (e.g. enjoying a massage), olfactory (e.g. aromas), taste (e.g. a sweet flavour), or cerebral (e.g. the 'buzz' from a psychoactive drug or being amused).

To experience pleasant sights and sounds: To receive aesthetic pleasure from things that we can see or hear (e.g. visual art, natural beauty, and music).

To be healthy: To feel well and know that our body is functioning as it should.

To own things: To possess objects, land, money and even, in some cases, people.

To be mentally stimulated: To have experiences that engage our thought processes (e.g. puzzles, entertainment, hobbies).

To feel secure: To feel confident that our needs will be met now and in the future.

To feel fulfilled: To have goals that are being met.

To feel self-respect: To think well of ourselves.

To feel agency: To feel in control of our destiny and actions.

To feel competent: To feel that we are good at things we value.

To discover things: To acquire new information and understanding.

To express ourselves: To externalise our feelings whether or not there is someone to hear or see us.

To have a higher purpose: To feel that we are taking part in a plan or contributing to objectives that extend beyond ourselves, whether spiritual, social or physical.

Jamie Okay, let's turn to the last category: common *social wants and needs.*

Robert These are all to do with interacting with other people. Basically, these are feelings of empathy, affection, trust, belonging, dominance, obedience, reciprocity, recognition, popularity and fairness. Every one of these can create powerful wants and needs.

Jamie Ah, the stuff of great plays!

Robert It's the stuff of life. People have written plenty of books on each. For the purposes of this chapter, I just want to acknowledge them so we realise they're important influences on our behaviour.

Social Sources Of Wants And Needs

To be loved: To have another person, or other people, feel love for us.

To have a life partner: To feel psychologically bonded with another person in a secure, lasting, intimate relationship.

To be liked: To have other people like us.

To be useful: To be able to meet other people's wants and needs.

To be valued: To have other people ascribe worth to us because of who we are, what we are like or what we do.

To inform people: To tell/teach people about things.

To have authority over people: To have other people do what we want.

To perform a role: To perform actions that are part of a role that we have accepted.

To obey orders: To do things that we are told to do by an authority.

To be better than other people: To perform better, have higher status, own more and generally be 'worth' more than other people.

To feel empathy: To experience and care about other people's feelings.

To be known: To have other people know who we are.

To be private: To avoid other people having personal information about us.

To belong: To feel that we are an accepted part of a group.

To be respected: To have other people regard us highly.

To feel connected: To feel that we share experiences and attributes with other people.

To protect people we care about: To prevent people we care about coming to harm.

To make other people feel better: To comfort other people if they feel bad or to make them feel good.

To show reciprocity: To give to the extent that we receive and vice versa.

To see fairness: To see people receive from other people, or the world in general, what we believe to be their due, including seeing 'justice' done.

Jamie So, we've got all these sources of wants and needs. How do they fit in with our animal brain?

Robert As you may have guessed, these sources of wants and needs come from a mixture of both our animal and human brain. The two are intimately entwined. So, imagine you feel hungry and you start contemplating your options for lunch. Here, the animal brain is first in the chain, followed by the human brain. However, you could also imagine a scenario where your human brain has decided on a specific diet – for example, let's say you've been a vegetarian for the last ten years. This framework will dictate what you want to eat.

Jamie And that would be the human brain first in the chain.

Robert Again, this is a simplification, but it's useful to illustrate how our human and animal brains interact.

Jamie Okay, what I really want to know is how can we make use of these sources of wants and needs – both in terms of managing ourselves and others?

Robert Good question. Although humans share a huge amount in common, we can have different wants and needs – or at least prioritise our wants and needs in a different order. Some people crave financial security and will take on a job they're not especially keen on to meet that need. Others might crave an interesting job and can put up with the discomfort of not having a lot of money in the bank.

Jamie I've noticed it's very easy for us to project our wants and needs onto other people. We assume they want what we want.

Robert Exactly. The typical mistake people make is to assume that someone else is driven by exactly the same things as themselves. So, if you care about maximising the company turnover, you might try to motivate your workers by emphasising this point because it's something that would motivate you. But actually, the team might care more about the quality of the product, receiving praise, or the possibility of an extra day off.

Jamie The ex-England cricket captain Michael Vaughan talked about this in terms of motivating his players. So, some players might care a lot about their statistics, which means they could be motivated by having a record on the horizon that they could break. Others might care more about money, so they might be particularly driven by personal financial incentives.

Robert The key is to observe people and communicate with them in order to understand what motivates them. Don't just make assumptions based on your own wants and needs.

Jamie So, if I'm trying to motivate someone else, I could go through our list of wants and needs and see which ones might apply to the person I'm trying to change?

Robert Yes. It can act as a prompt to get you thinking outside of yourself.

Jamie Ah – but I'm also thinking I could do the same thing to better understand how I can motivate myself.

Robert Indeed. Try to figure out what genuinely motivates you. Don't feel you *should* be motivated by the same things as people you see around you or in the media.

Jamie   To quote Monty Python's *Life of Brian*: 'We're all individuals!'

Robert   (*laughs*) Well, what's interesting is that when I started developing the list of wants and needs, I called it 'Universal sources of wants and needs', but fairly quickly I had to change it to 'Common sources of wants and needs'. There's a huge amount of variety in humans about what things really matter to us. It's likely for a good reason because a society needs a certain amount of diversity to thrive. But it can also feel validating to see that your wants and needs are, in fact, common – even if people around you might think otherwise.

Jamie   I think it can be strange when you compare yourself to other people and realise that what makes them tick just doesn't work for you. I have a strong need to express myself artistically and an ambition to push myself. But when I'm around people who, quite naturally, don't feel that way, I can start to feel a bit like a weirdo!

Robert   Right. Learning about these wants and needs can be normalising and provide comfort – which is, of course, one of our basic wants and needs!

KEY POINTS

- There are a huge number of important wants and needs which can often conflict with each other.

- Our sources of wants and needs fall into three overlapping categories: *biological, psychological* and *social.*

- Some needs are universal, like the need for oxygen, nutrition and rest. Others are important to most people but not all, like the need for sex.

- If you're trying to influence other people, think about what wants and needs matter to them. Don't assume they prioritise their wants and needs in the same way as you.

- If you're trying to motivate yourself, browse the sources of wants and needs and see which ones you care about most. This can help guide you when developing strategies to achieve your goals.

6. Influencing The Animal Brain

Jamie I want to talk a little bit more about how we can influence the animal brain. You mentioned before that it responds strongly to images. Are there other effective techniques for getting the animal brain to do what we want?

Robert Well, let's start by acknowledging that there are moments when it's very difficult to control the animal brain – times when emotions are running hot, and the stakes feel very high.

Jamie Yes! I remember a gig I played where, after the show, one of the audience members refused to leave the venue and started throwing insults at the bouncer. The bouncer, who was gigantic, eventually lost his temper and made a lunge for the guy. It took five people to hold him back. They kept trying to talk him down, but he was completely blinded by fury. Worse still, the audience member kept taunting him and had to be dragged away by his friends before things got really ugly!

Robert I daresay alcohol may have been involved. In extreme circumstances like that, a physical intervention may be required. And removing the provoking stimuli can be useful – in this case, separating the people and moving them a long way from each other.

Jamie It was pretty frightening.

Robert I can imagine. That's an example where the animal brain has completely taken over. However, there are many situations where the animal brain is not bothered by events in the present moment – it feels relatively safe and comfortable. Recognising these moments is key because the human brain can use this time to form plans and strategies that can influence the animal brain in more heated or high stakes situations in the future.

Jamie So, we need to influence the animal brain during periods of calm?

Robert Exactly. Think of Odysseus and the Sirens' song –

Jamie Oh, good – a modern example.

Robert The Sirens' song was said to be so beautiful that it drove sailors mad and lured them to shipwreck on the rocks. Odysseus was determined to hear the song and live to tell the tale.

Jamie Okay...

Robert So, before he reached the Sirens, Odysseus was not susceptible to their charms which meant he could take action to prevent himself from being seduced by them later. In this case, that meant getting his crew to tie him to the ship's mast.

Jamie So, when he hears the Sirens' song, he goes temporarily mad with desire, but he can't shipwreck the boat.

YES, I CAN SEE HOW THIS COULD DRIVE YOU MAD

ODYSSEUS TRIES EXPOSURE THERAPY

Robert And to take a more ordinary, real-world example – if you want to change some part of your behaviour, you can make a plan when you're feeling relatively relaxed and comfortable. In that state, you can devise strategies for how you'll respond in moments when your emotions are triggered.

Jamie I imagine not being under threat allows you to think more widely or objectively, right? So you can problem-solve better.

Robert Indeed. And sometimes it's useful to do this with another person, either formally or informally. With formal counselling, the counsellor creates a safe, non-emotionally reactive environment. And in that space, the client can prepare for challenging situations and practise responding in different ways.

Jamie   Kind of like a rehearsal?

Robert   Roleplaying an upcoming scenario can be a very useful technique. It might be something as simple as rehearsing a response to someone offering you a cigarette at a party. So, you might practice the line, 'No thanks, I've given up,' several times. And your counsellor will reward you so that it feels good to do the new behaviour. That way, you've trained your animal brain for the pressured moment later on.

Jamie   You're rewarding the behaviour you want in the rehearsal itself?

Robert   Absolutely. And with virtual reality technology, you can take this rehearsal to a whole new level. You can guide people through quite realistic scenarios and slowly help them to overcome phobias or deal with traumas, for example. Rehearsal is crucial for training your animal brain, and we'll talk more about it in the chapter on building habits.

Jamie   Okay. How else can we influence the animal brain during these periods of planning?

Robert   You might want to think about what emotion you want to elicit.

Jamie   Go on...

Robert   Professor Val Curtis, a wonderful British behavioural scientist – sadly no longer with us – did some great work with her colleagues on improving hygiene practices in places like Burkina Faso and Peru. Essentially, they discovered that simply providing information about the importance of washing hands wasn't enough to get people to change their behaviour. They needed to actually provoke *disgust* around the idea of having been in contact with faeces.

Jamie So, here, they're not just using facts and figures. They're deliberately trying to elicit a strong emotion.

Robert And obviously different emotions have different qualities. Disgust doesn't habituate over time – meaning we don't get used to it – whereas anxiety over faecal matter causing disease does.

Jamie And anxiety is a form of fear, which I'm assuming is useful in other contexts.

Robert Fear is a powerful tool to control behaviour and affect the animal brain. But you have to be careful because, as I say, we can get used to people saying frightening things to us. That means if you're trying to control people using anxiety, you have to keep upping the threat level.

Jamie That's fascinating. I've noticed news websites seem to thrive on escalating conflicts or problems. And no sooner has one story been resolved than another even more frightening one comes along. It's like they're trying to keep us in a perpetual state of fear. Do we really get used to that?

Robert In a way, we do. Not to the extent that we read headlines without feeling anxious, obviously. But, remember, they're presenting us with the worst events happening across the globe. Our response may be, 'I feel pretty bad,' but usually terrible news stories don't completely overwhelm our day.

Jamie True. Occasionally, stories break through that really upset me personally, but, most of the time, it's quite a low-level thrumming fear.

Robert And I should point out there are many good journalists doing valuable work and bringing important issues to our attention. It's not all scaremongering.

Jamie I agree. But I'm not keen on them frightening us just to keep us returning to their websites so they can stay in business.

Robert That's another useful thing to think about: what kind of stimuli do you expose yourself to? What emotions do you want to evoke in yourself? It's unlikely your animal brain will be totally unaffected by casually reading news stories about brutal murders.

Jamie I suppose it's obvious when you put it like that!

Robert We can also use images or other stimuli to influence *drive states*, which we talked about earlier. For example, adverts featuring juicy burgers that ooze ketchup and mayonnaise.

Jamie I'm getting hungry just hearing about it.

Robert And think about the number of film trailers featuring clips of semi-nudity – engaging our sex drive, of course.

Jamie So, we might want to think about what drive states we can elicit from the animal brain.

Robert And, again, we can consider this in relation to our own and other people's behaviour. For example, if you're on a diet, you may want to avoid stimuli that tap into the hunger drive. Of course, if you're a restauranteur trying to attract customers, you'll have the opposite motive!

Jamie Nice. So, being aware of how the animal brain can be influenced means we can be more conscious of the way other people are trying to affect our behaviour.

Robert Absolutely – that's key.

Jamie Any other tips for influencing the animal brain?

Robert You can take advantage of the way the animal brain does something called *associative learning*. We looked at this a bit earlier with our discussion on operant conditioning, which is a type of associative learning. When mental events occur close to each other in time, the brain forms a connection between them. For example, saying 'peek-a-boo' to a baby, seeing them laugh and then feeling good creates a connection in our brains, so we feel anticipated pleasure at the thought of saying 'peek-a-boo' again. It's why we learn to like things that have good associations and dislike things with bad associations.

Jamie Ah, so if we want someone to think positively about something, like our company or product, we associate it with something they already like?

Robert That's exactly right and one reason that companies use likeable, celebrity ambassadors.

Jamie Such as Usain Bolt.

Robert Yes. Because he's a charismatic and successful athlete, companies that use him in adverts are hoping some of the positive emotion will spill over onto their product. In addition, the celebrity acts as a kind of 'trustworthy' source.

Jamie If you want people to like your product or message, you can associate it with something your audience already likes.

Robert Yep. With celebrity endorsements, you're often building an association between a positive role model and something you want people to feel positively about. Sometimes they can get so intertwined it can be difficult to separate them.

Jamie I always feel a bit unnerved when a sports star switches clothing brands. Part of me is convinced their success has been down to their fancy Nike clothes.

Robert (*laughs*) Another option is to play on existing associations. For example, we naturally have an association between seeing a starving child and feeling pity. You don't need to teach your audience to connect those two things. It's one reason starving children are portrayed in charity adverts, appealing to our sense of pity to motivate us to make a donation. So, when you're creating an advert or a product, it's worth considering what associations your audience already has and seeing if you can work with those.

Jamie I feel we've covered a lot of ground quickly. Let me see if I can recap: it's easier to make plans to influence the animal brain when we're in a relatively calm state. During this time, we can rehearse and reward the behaviours we want. We can also think about what emotion or drive state we want to elicit using the appropriate stimuli. Finally, we can take advantage of associative learning to get the animal brain to like new things, as well as taking advantage of existing associations.

Robert Correct. There's a lot of powerful techniques in this chapter, but once you've got your head around them, you can use them in so many different situations. You'll also find your ability to influence your own and other people's animal brains greatly increases.

KEY POINTS

- When emotions run high, it can be hard to influence the animal brain.

- If you're trying to change behaviour, pick a time when the animal brain is relatively calm and relaxed. During this period, it's easier to plan for situations when the animal brain is likely to take over.

- Rehearse the behaviour you want to perform ahead of time and reward it.

- Consider what emotion or drive state you want to elicit from the animal brain – for example, disgust, hunger etc.

- *Associative learning* is when two events occur close to each other so the brain forms a connection between them.

- If you want people to like your product, pair it with something your audience already likes.

- Think about what pre-existing associations your audience already has and how you can use them to influence the animal brain.

7. Impulses And Inhibitions

Jamie   So, we've talked about how wants and needs are crucial in terms of understanding our animal and human brains, and we've looked at ways to influence the animal brain. What's next?

Robert There's another fundamental pair of psychological forces we need to discuss: *impulses* and *inhibitions*.

Jamie   Okay, what's an impulse?

Robert It's hard to describe in any terms other than biological, but I'll give it a go. You can think of an impulse as the immediate precursor to literally *every* behaviour. It's the pattern of activation of nerve pathways in the brain that, if not countered, will cause your muscles to make the behaviour happen.

Jamie   So impulses are behind all our actions, not just so-called 'impulsive' ones?

Robert That's right. We talk about impulsive behaviour when we act without thinking first – like buying something online without actually considering it. But impulses underlie every single one of our actions. They're the building blocks of behaviour. They operate in planned behaviours too, by which I mean actions that we have thought about first. It's just that, there, the impulses are being driven by our thoughts.

Jamie   I take it we can't always be aware of our impulses?

Robert Most of the time we're not. Sometimes, smokers will find themselves lighting up a cigarette even though there's one still burning in the ashtray. It's become an automatic behaviour.

Jamie Or like changing gears when I'm driving. I'm not consciously thinking about it, my body has just learned to do it.

Robert And, often, what you can observe is the result of the impulse – in this case, changing gears. But you can't observe the impulse itself.

Jamie You've lost me.

Robert I mean that you can't actually see the neurons firing in your brain. Most of the time you don't actually feel anything when you have an impulse to do something because it's so automatic. But sometimes you can feel what we call an *urge*.

Jamie An urge? I think I had one of those as a teenager...

Robert (*laughs*) An urge is the feeling you get when an impulse is *frustrated* in some way. This might be because you're deliberately stopping yourself from doing the behaviour or because something else is stopping you from doing it. So when smokers have an urge to smoke, the urge is produced because the impulse to light up is being thwarted. This might be because they're trying to quit so they're trying to stop themselves from smoking or because they're in an environment where smoking is not allowed.

Jamie Or they've run out of cigarettes.

Robert That's another possibility.

Jamie Let me check I'm with you so far: impulses drive all of our behaviours, and we're largely unconscious of them in the same way we're usually unconscious of our hearts pumping blood around our bodies. However, if an impulse to do something is frustrated, we can sometimes experience a feeling of tension, which is what we call an 'urge'.

Robert Perfect.

Jamie And what's the difference between a want and an urge?

Robert Wants are feelings of attraction to any kind of imagined future, but they are not necessarily linked to any *specific* behaviour. So, I might want a new guitar, but until I walk past a guitar shop and see a particular model I like, I won't have an urge to buy one.

Jamie Sometimes I feel like I have an urge to buy *something*, I just don't know what it is yet!

Robert (*laughs*) Yes, of course that's possible. And it's doubly frustrating because you don't even know what you want. I know from teaching students about this that people find it confusing – but urges always relate to a feeling of being compelled to carry out an action *right now*. And it focuses exclusively on the action, not the consequences of the action.

Jamie Can we just come back to 'impulsive' behaviour? People usually use the term to describe someone suddenly behaving rashly, badly, or in a way that's out of character. I find when I'm performing a song onstage, I can be pretty impulsive, and I might suddenly decide to walk out into the audience or grab a drumstick and play my guitar with it. What's going on in these situations?

Robert That brings us on to the other side of that particular coin: inhibition. When we talk about 'impulsive behaviour', we're talking about people doing things without thinking it through first. Now, part of what thinking does is to stop us doing stupid things. It acts to inhibit our actions. And I know this sounds boring, but inhibition is absolutely crucial to living happy, productive lives.

Jamie But uninhibited behaviour can be fun...

Robert Only up to a point. By and large, if we always do things we feel like doing when we feel like doing them, it doesn't turn out well!

Jamie So, this kind of impulsive behaviour I'm describing is due to a lack of inhibitions. And sometimes that can be great, like when it helps spice up a live performance, but it can also be dangerous – for example, speeding through a traffic light.

Robert Yep.

Jamie And how do inhibitions develop?

Robert Imagine you're a child and you see another child playing with a toy you want. You go over and snatch it out of their hands. Your teacher sees this, scolds you, and gives the toy back to the child. Over time, you form the idea that it would be 'wrong' to snatch toys from other children. So, after a time, when you see other children playing with their toys, you may experience the urge to take it from them – which involves a feeling of tension – but the inhibition has been created.

Jamie You're describing a process of socialisation. I suppose that's what a lot of it is – avoiding acting purely on our own impulses without considering others.

Robert But inhibitions are about a lot more than just stopping this so-called 'impulsive' behaviour.

Jamie Ah, of course. Because impulses underlie all our actions, it makes sense that we need a broader understanding of how inhibitions work too, and not just in relation to 'impulsive' behaviour.

Robert You're catching on! We use inhibitions pretty much all the time. Whenever you have an impulse to do more than one thing, your brain has to pick one and stop you doing the others – otherwise your muscles would get very confused. For example, when you're driving and you approach amber traffic lights, you have to decide whether to press the accelerator or move your foot over to the brake. Let's say you decide to brake – your brain has to inhibit the impulse to simply press your foot down. This is normally automatic, but it can go wrong, and accidents have happened because the driver slammed their foot on the accelerator rather than moving it to the brake and then pressing down.

Jamie Is this about me driving your Ford Focus?

Robert You tell me.

Jamie It was 15 years ago, and the wall appeared out of nowhere! Anyway, I take your point – we're using inhibitions a lot.

Robert Right. So, when someone acts 'impulsively', we're talking about a failure of the inhibition system. But we use the inhibition system all the time to stop ourselves trying to perform two competing actions simultaneously.

Jamie It's funny, I've been thinking about impulses and impulsive behaviour in relation to 'wild' or dangerous behaviour. But, actually, when you look at our work culture, many of us – especially freelancers and people working from home – struggle to stop working. This could mean working through lunch or not logging off until late in the evening. It's very hard to regulate oneself.

Robert Indeed. And part of that is how our impulses and urges are affected by social rewards and punishments. If your boss expects you to answer emails at three in the morning, that will undoubtably contribute to the problem!

Jamie So, stopping things is actually quite complicated. But what about the opposite? I'm thinking about times when I've struggled to *start* doing something.

Robert Good point. There are people suffering with depression who find it very hard to start doing things. Their inhibition system is either too strong or their impulses are not strong enough. Obviously, there are usually many factors in play with depression, but at a very basic, building blocks level, that's one of the things going on.

Jamie I see. Going back a moment, we talked about the social influence on inhibitions – does that mean all inhibitions are learned?

Robert No – they're a mixture. Simply switching from one behaviour to another involves inhibition, so our body is inhibiting behaviours right from the beginning – obviously not necessarily consciously.

Jamie Like when a baby is crying and the parent tries to cheer them up by waving a toy in their face. You can see a little tussle going on inside the baby as it moves from crying to being entertained!

Robert And we can train – and possibly override – our impulses too.

Jamie Like how you can stop yourself breathing for a bit.

Robert Or control the speed and depth of your breathing.

Jamie Have you got any other examples of this training?

Robert Well, one way to view habits is to think of them as learned impulses.

Jamie Go on ...

Robert So, for example, washing your hands before preparing food. That isn't something that's built in by nature, we have to learn to do that.

Jamie And for centuries, we didn't truly know the importance of hygiene. I only found out the other day that the sewage system wasn't built in London until the 19th century!

Robert Yes, before that the Thames was an open sewer! But these days, almost everyone preparing food will have been taught and developed the habit of washing their hands before handling ingredients. And the stimulus might be as simple as getting the vegetables out of the cupboard and that prompting them to wash their hands.

Jamie So, it's an unconscious habit – like brushing your teeth and showering first thing in the morning.

Robert Even going for a shower involves a lot of learned impulses. You just don't have to think about them – at least not very much.

Jamie Which is why we can be absent-minded and not remember if we have actually brushed our teeth, or whatever.

Robert Exactly.

Jamie So, we've got impulses, inhibitions, and learned impulses. There's a lot going on. How do we decide which impulses to follow?

Robert Think of it this way: there is a constant battle between impulses arising and inhibitions stopping them. And the behaviour we actually do is the result of the strongest impulse that is going on at the time.

Jamie Ah, does this tie in with your oft-repeated phrase: 'We always act in pursuit of what we most want or need at that exact moment'?

Robert It does! Imagine your manager has come over to your desk to criticise a piece of work you've done. They're mean, you feel bad. But, on their way out, you see them trip and almost fall over a chair . . .

Jamie Oh, no ...

Robert So you're going to feel an intense impulse to laugh.

Jamie Oh, yes ...

Robert But your boss is still in earshot. So, there is a conflict between your impulse to laugh and your desire to keep your job, or not get into trouble, which creates an inhibition. And whichever is the strongest out of the impulse and the inhibition will determine what you do in that moment.

Jamie I'm thinking I might just cover my mouth and try to disguise my laugh as a cough.

Robert Sometimes the laughter just comes out! You can't control it.

Jamie (*laughs*) I think laughter and inhibitions are very interesting. In comedy clubs, at the start of a night, the audience is often awkward and quiet. It takes a bit of time for the crowd to 'warm up'. But after that, they'll laugh hysterically at jokes they may otherwise, and in a different context, find totally inappropriate. It's as though they have permission to let their inhibitions down and laugh. I guess that's the purpose of a comedy club.

Robert Not to mention that comedy clubs usually serve alcohol, which lowers inhibitions. Although times change and what is permissible to laugh at, even in comedy clubs, will change along with prevailing attitudes.

Jamie The inhibitions around certain topics increase.

Robert Yes, or the impulse to laugh simply isn't there anymore because the material just seems crass or offensive to the audience.

Jamie Okay, let's get back onto the main track. You've said that whichever is stronger, our impulses or inhibitions, will dictate what we do in a particular moment. I'm imagining our wants and needs must feed into this.

Robert Yes. Our wants and needs act as an important input to the impulse-inhibition mechanism.

Jamie How do you mean?

Robert Well, seeing a box of ice cream in the supermarket acts as an external stimulus, which affects your wants and needs. This, in turn, affects your impulses and inhibitions.

Jamie Can the want arise without an external stimulus?

Robert Yes, and we talked about this in relation to the homeostatic processes earlier. There, the body wants to get us to a certain state so, for example, if we need food, we'll experience hunger. But thoughts and images can also simply arise in our minds, creating wants and needs.

Jamie I might happen to be daydreaming of ice-cream – perhaps because I'm hungry – and that creates a want and then an impulse to go out and buy one.

Robert Yes. It's funny when we put it into concrete examples because it can feel like stuff we already know. And in a way we do. But learning about these basic building blocks helps us when we want to understand and change behaviour.

Jamie Well, that's exactly what I want to do. In particular, I'm interested in how we develop these learned impulses, or habits, as the rest of us call them.

Robert You're in luck because that's the topic of our next chapter.

KEY POINTS

- An *impulse* is the immediate precursor to *every* behaviour. It's the activation of nerve pathways in the brain that, if uninhibited, leads to behaviour.

- Most impulses are unconscious.

- An *urge* is a frustrated impulse. It occurs when you feel compelled to carry out an action right now, but something is stopping you.

- *Inhibitions* stop us performing actions, and they're operating constantly. In order to do one action, our bodies need to stop us doing any other action.

- *Habits* can be thought of as learned impulses – for example, learning to wash our hands before preparing food.

- There is a constant battle between impulses arising and inhibitions stopping them. The behaviour we actually do is the result of whichever is the strongest impulse in the moment.

8. How To Build Habits

Jamie   I want to learn how to put some of this theory into practice. Let's talk about how we can harness our animal brain to build habits.

Robert   Okay. The main thing to reiterate is that impulses literally underpin all of our behaviour. So, when we're trying to cultivate a behaviour, we need to make sure that the impulse to do it is stronger than any other impulses or inhibitions that are going on.

Jamie   Million-dollar question: how do we do that?

Robert   Essentially, we need to use our human brain to train our animal brain into forming habits we want. Don't worry, we'll be looking at plenty of practical tips in this chapter.

Jamie   And the undercurrent is that we can often end up falling into unhealthy habits, right? Binge-reading unpleasant news stories, snacking on junk food . . .

Robert   Yes, forming unhealthy habits is a lot easier to do because our animal brain is tuned to learn from immediate rewards. Unfortunately, these can often be harmful to us in the long run. And, as we discussed earlier, social media and news websites also use unpredictable intermittent rewards to control our behaviour, and this works on us in a very powerful way.

Jamie   So, that's what we're up against. Let's dive in! You said that we could think of habits as learned impulses.

Robert Yes, they are learned stimulus-impulse associations. As with most of our technical terms, it sounds complicated but it refers to something that's actually quite simple. You come home from work and see the TV remote – this is the stimulus. You then have an impulse to press the button to switch the TV on. And of course, this is behaviour you've learned, probably from a parent or sibling. Our lives are made up of habits of all kinds: healthy, unhealthy and neutral.

Jamie So, just turning a door handle is a habit?

Robert Indeed. Not a very interesting one but quite important for getting in and out of rooms.

Jamie And how do you train a new habit?

Robert First, define what habit you want to train as specifically as possible. For example: writing for half an hour after breakfast on weekday mornings.

Jamie I think that's an easy step to miss or leave vague. So, I might say to myself, 'I want to write more' but not necessarily consider what that might mean in practical terms.

Robert Sometimes open goals can be helpful. But in terms of building habits, it's generally useful to be specific.

Jamie Okay, what's the next step of the training?

Robert Repetition and more repetition.

Jamie Like drilling army soldiers?

Robert That's right. Drills instil and reinforce a particular behaviour so when a soldier finds themself in a particular situation, they perform the behaviour that has been drilled.

Jamie We all know the cliché of the intimidating sergeant.

Robert And that sergeant is getting the soldiers to repeat a particular behaviour, or set of behaviours, by barking orders.

Jamie So, the soldiers obey to begin with because they'll get punished otherwise?

Robert Yes. The sergeant uses the threat of punishment to drill the solders. But the soldiers also accept the sergeant's authority – it's part of the deal when they sign up.

Jamie Tough love.

Robert Love might be putting it strongly.

Jamie You know, my drama teacher used to tell us that acting on stage was like taking a driving test. She'd go round saying, *'Practise, practise, practise!'* Her reasoning was that when the time came to perform, we'd be very nervous. So we had to get the words and movements 'into the body', so to speak. That way, despite the nerves, our bodies would know what to do.

Robert Did it work?

Jamie Very much so. Both for my driving test and acting onstage! It's easy to underestimate how different your body can feel under pressure – the thumping heart, brain fog and sweaty hands. That's why, personally, I often like to rehearse a little bit more than feels sensible.

Robert Rehearsing is extremely important, particularly in situations of heightened emotion and threat when you might freeze or hesitate. At those times, you need to do something without thinking, and this is where *overlearning* comes in handy.

DRIVING SCHOOL BOOT CAMP

Jamie So, in those scenarios, the animal brain takes over and you can perform the behaviour with little or no thought?

Robert Yes. And, interestingly, if the human brain gets too involved, it can actually inhibit high performance.

Jamie Every actor has had the experience of suddenly feeling self-conscious onstage and struggling to remember what they're supposed to do next.

Robert I think anyone who's ever had to stand up and do a presentation at school or work will know the feeling as well.

Jamie But what about the other side of the argument? Sometimes over-rehearsing can make a show feel dull or stilted. Contrary to what I just said, there are other times I deliberately under-rehearse so that I can be more impulsive on stage and leave room for exciting things to happen.

Robert Good point. Different scenarios call for different amounts and types of rehearsal.

Jamie So, repetition is crucial to building habits, and it may involve a certain amount of reward and punishment. Now, how about building *healthy* habits?

Robert Well, one way to do this is to tweak existing habits to fit your longer-term goals.

Jamie Okay ...

Robert Let's say that there are triggers for an existing habit in your environment. For example, you have a high cupboard in your kitchen where you store crisps.

Jamie You know about that?!

Robert (*laughs*) You can make a simple tweak here and replace the crisps with a healthier snack, like rice cakes or popcorn, or even just smaller sized packets. It depends on what your goal is and the best way of working with yourself to achieve that.

Jamie There's a show on TV called *Eat Well For Less* where they swap families' usual unhealthy or expensive food for healthier, cheaper options.

Robert Sounds sensible.

Jamie But here's the thing – they get rid of all the labels and branding! So, essentially, it's just down to the taste of the product. And it's fascinating because so many people on it make a point of talking about 'their' brand at the start of the show and how they'll know, without a doubt, if the product's been swapped. But once the label's off the tin, they often can't tell. A lot of the time, they actually end up preferring the cheaper, supermarket brand.

Robert I think I could tell if my coffee had been swapped.

Jamie They all begin the same way! Anyway, I made a few changes to my shop after watching the show, trying out cheaper or healthier options. And it's worked well so far. I think because it's just a simple swap, as you say, it doesn't require much conscious thought.

Robert That's a perfect example of looking at your environment and tweaking triggers to train healthier habits. Alternatively, you could put new triggers into your environment so that they'll prompt you to do the behaviour you want.

Jamie Go on...

Robert So, let's say you want to get into the habit of going to the gym on Sunday morning but you're struggling to do it. What would you do?

Jamie I would … set my alarm to the *Rocky* theme tune?

Robert (*laughs*) Not bad! You could also lay out your gym clothes on a chair the night before. This will not only provide a visual cue for you but it means that a practical barrier to exercising – i.e. finding your kit – will have already been taken out of the equation.

Jamie So, this is the human brain making a plan because it knows the animal brain will just want to stay in bed and sleep. It's Odysseus sailing past the Sirens again.

Robert Exactly.

Jamie Talking about putting triggers in the environment, I have guitars on stands in a few rooms in the house so I can simply pick up and play them. I love playing guitar, but I definitely play more with visual cues reminding me – and, of course, it takes away the barrier of getting them out of a case. Frankly, I try not to use my will-power if I don't have to.

Robert If you can change your environment to make it easier to perform a desired behaviour, do it! Understanding how to manipulate your environment and bolster your habits is a very important self-regulatory skill. It also feeds into our sense of agency, fulfilment and self-respect.

Jamie I think it's also tricky because it's not one size fits all. I feel like I'm constantly making adjustments to my routine, my environment and habits to get myself to do the things I want on a regular basis. Sometimes it can be challenging to figure out what works and what doesn't.

Robert And, of course, circumstances change, and then new habits need to be created. It's not like a wind-up toy that you can just let loose.

Jamie So maintaining habits is a dynamic process.

Robert Exactly.

Jamie How long does it takes to form a habit?

Robert It depends on the activity, the environment and the individual. But it will generally get easier each time. As we saw earlier, it's important to give the animal brain a little reward immediately after the behaviour at first. Then, over time, the behaviour can become rewarding in and of itself. You're trying to get to a state where you don't have to think about whether or not doing the behaviour is a good idea – you just do it.

Jamie I've heard that advice before. My problem is that it can veer into the sentiment, 'Just force yourself to get on with it.' And sometimes that works, but, just as often, the habit breaks down.

Robert You're right. While the 'force yourself' mentality can work, it can be coercive. And it's often coupled with a lack of reward after we've completed the habit, which can make it doubly punishing.

Jamie That's exactly what happens! I've found this with writing sometimes. I'll try to force myself to do it, then punish myself afterwards with phrases like, 'Well, turning up is the bare minimum I expect of myself!' It's a misguided attempt at motivating myself.

Robert I bet it makes you less likely to want to come back tomorrow?

Jamie Very much so. But after learning about how the animal brain works, I'm beginning to appreciate how powerful and important rewards are. When you think about it, who wants to work if they get punished after they've completed a task? As I mentioned earlier, I had to build the practice of giving myself a lot of praise after I'd written something.

Robert Praise is so crucial. We can sometimes think we've outgrown the need for praise when we become adults, but it's not true. Praising ourselves continues to be very important.

Jamie Sometimes, I still slip back into old ways of thinking. But, overall, I'm having a much better hit-rate, and – surprise, surprise – I *feel* much better.

Robert That's the thing, it's not rocket science. But we have to overcome our previous ways of trying to get ourselves, or other people, to do things. Often, this means less stick and more carrot. But also making sure we pick the right carrot – so, something *genuinely* motivating!

Jamie How else can we build habits?

Robert Well, it's important to remember that habits don't take place in isolation. And this means that you can string habits together.

Jamie How so?

Robert Let's say you want to stretch more regularly to help with aches and pains.

Jamie I'm getting to that age.

Robert Join the club. So, perhaps you already go to the gym, but you usually just jump straight onto the treadmill or start doing weights. One option might be to add in five minutes of stretching at the beginning and end of your workout. That means you don't have to form an entirely new habit – you've piggybacked on what's currently there.

Jamie I've heard that referred to as 'stacking' habits. Does it work?

Robert It's very handy because it just stops you having to add a new, totally separate activity into your day. Starting and stopping often require willpower. So stringing habits together, or 'stacking' them, can ease the burden.

Jamie I'm guessing that a routine is useful too. Say, brushing your teeth 30 minutes after breakfast?

Robert Absolutely. And you'll notice if you don't brush your teeth – because, say, something interrupted your routine – you may not feel quite right until you've done it.

Jamie You're right – it's uncomfortable.

Robert Your mouth may not feel fresh, or you may feel bad about not doing something that you know you should have done. Or you might just feel 'a bit off'.

Jamie I know a lot of our readers, like us, will have quite complicated lives and haphazard routines. Sometimes it just isn't possible to do things at the same time each day.

Robert The key here is to be able to improvise, and, again, this means being prepared. During the COVID-19 outbreak, we had to wear a mask going into stores. So, I made a small COVID kit with a fresh mask, hand sanitiser and a pack of tissues, and made sure it was in my coat pocket whenever I left the house.

Jamie Me too. Even if I didn't think I was going to go into a shop, I'd take it with me to give me options if I changed my mind.

Robert Planning and being prepared can really help us to build better habits. And technology is very useful here, too.

Jamie Now more than ever. I made the switch a few years back to working in 'the cloud', which meant I could just carry a slimline keyboard and work off my phone when I had a spare half an hour, out and about.

Robert Ah ha! So now you have the capability to take advantage of an opportunity.

Jamie Back to the *COM-B* model we discussed in *Energise*, our first book in this series. Capability, Opportunity and Motivation all feed into directing our Behaviour.

Robert I'm impressed you remembered it.

Jamie So am I!

Robert You introduced me to using a habit app a while back which I use to track the different habits I do and how often I do them. I find ticking the habit off to be very rewarding.

Jamie I know exactly what you mean. When I first downloaded it, I got, uh... a little over enthusiastic and began loading myself up with all the habits I had to do each day. After a while, I realised that it was beginning to become quite punishing. Not the app itself but the way I was using it.

Robert What did you do then?

Jamie I had to have a think about why I'd installed it and what my actual medium and long-term goals were. And this helped me realise I didn't have to do every habit every day in order to make progress. And now I try to use the app as a source of data and a gentle encouragement to do behaviours that are important to me.

Robert That's the thing. As a stats nerd, I have to say that data is very useful. It's not a reliance on memory or feelings, it's a real record of what you've actually done.

Jamie Yeah, I'm frequently surprised looking over my habits. Sometimes I feel I haven't played guitar in a while, but then I check my app and I played the day before.

Robert And there's lots of fancy tech that can give you a leg-up. My Fitbit certainly helps me to get more steps in the day and to keep an eye on how much I'm eating. Achieving 10,000 steps always feels like a real win.

Jamie I feel I should add a disclaimer for our tech-averse readers and say that you don't *need* any of this stuff to form healthy habits!

Robert (*laughs*) You certainly don't have to use any of these gadgets, but they can help.

Jamie So far, we've talked about habits as something we do alone – or with someone shouting at us! But other people can also help us to build habits right?

Robert Yes – if you find the right people and environment. Let's say you want to run more regularly, you might want to join a running club or find a training partner. Crucially, you want to collaborate with people who make it *more* likely you'll perform the desired habit.

Jamie (*laughs*) So, not the friend you'll end up staying in, ordering a pizza and watching TV with?

Robert Not on this occasion.

Jamie Is there anything else you want to add about building habits?

Robert The last thing I want to say is that sometimes your habit will be derailed – it's inevitable. So be prepared for setbacks, allow some flexibility into your plans, and try to get back to performing the habit where possible.

Jamie Sounds like good advice. I feel like we've covered a lot of ground, here. Can you sum up how we can develop good habits?

Robert I certainly can. Would you like a handy list of 11 key points?

Jamie Let's have it.

KEY POINTS SPECIAL:
How To Build A Habit

1. Make the habit specific – for example, write for 30 minutes five mornings a week.

2. Repetition is crucial.

3. Reward yourself after doing the habit.

4. Practise more before high pressure situations.

5. Modify existing habits by swapping in new behaviours.

6. Add triggers into your environment – for example, leaving your sports kit out.

7. String or 'stack' habits together – for example, flossing after brushing your teeth.

8. Try to form a regular routine.

9. If you have a haphazard routine, be prepared to do the habit when the opportunity arises.

10. Collaborate with others who are trying to build the same habit.

11. Prepare for setbacks, and get back to the habit where possible.

9. Reward vs Enjoyment

Jamie I want to talk a little more about *mindless* unhealthy habits because I often find myself scrolling endlessly on my phone or getting sucked into watching a string of random YouTube videos. I'm sure I could be using that time to do activities that are actually good for me, but I can't quite make it happen. So, what's going on there?

Robert Very good question. I think a lot of people are in a similar situation. What you're describing is engaging in behaviour that is rewarding but not enjoyable.

Jamie Aren't all rewards enjoyable?

Robert No. In everyday language, a 'reward' is given to someone in recognition of something they've achieved. Or we say something is 'rewarding' when it feels good. In psychology, the term 'reward' means something different and specific. We use it to describe an event or experience that motivates an animal to repeat the behaviour that preceded it.

Jamie So, when I'm scrolling on my phone, there's something in my brain that just says, 'repeat this behaviour'?

Robert That's right – and it doesn't have to be enjoyable.

Jamie This is taking me a moment to process. Tell me more . . .

Robert Take nicotine, the addictive drug in cigarettes. When smokers puff on a cigarette, they absorb nicotine into the bloodstream via their lungs and it goes very quickly to the brain. This causes a chemical called *dopamine* to be released. The release of dopamine tells the brain to pay attention to what the smoker was just doing – smoking a cigarette – and it also creates an association between the impulse to smoke and the situation the smoker was in.

Jamie Like smoking a cigarette after dinner?

Robert Exactly. So, next time the smoker finishes dinner, they'll feel an impulse to smoke. But, again, all this happens without the smoker needing to feel any pleasure at all.

Jamie You're saying smokers just 'think' they enjoy smoking?

Robert Some smokers really do enjoy smoking, of course. But, strange as it may seem, enjoyment is not primarily what's driving their urge to smoke.

Jamie The brain just says, 'Smoke!' whether or not it feels good? That doesn't seem like a very clever survival system.

Robert Well, cigarettes don't occur naturally in the environment! They're human-made. They hijack our animal brains, which generally evolved to deal with 'natural' rewards like food, drink, sex and bonding – things that are good for survival and reproduction.

Jamie I guess cigarettes are the opposite of that. But how do they hijack the brain?

Robert It's to do with a part of the animal brain called the *nucleus accumbens*, which controls how we respond to reward and punishment. I'm going to give you a slightly simplified explanation of how it operates, but it's a useful way to understand what we've just been talking about.

Jamie Is this explanation going to include pictures?

Robert Indeed, it will. So, the nucleus accumbens has two main parts: The *core* and the *shell*.

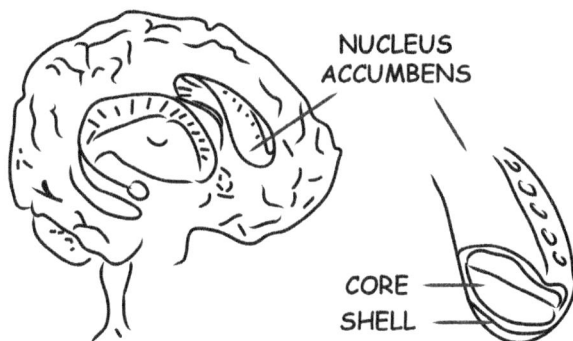

Jamie Let's start with the core.

Robert Okay. When dopamine is released in the core of the nucleus accumbens, it creates the association I was just talking about. It tells the brain to notice what you were just doing – in our example, it was smoking after dinner. Then, the next time you're in the same situation, you'll experience an impulse to do that same behaviour.

Jamie And the impulse doesn't need to feel good?

Robert It's pure psychological reward, no enjoyment necessary. It just says to the brain, 'Do it again.'

Jamie Nicotine releases dopamine in the core of the nucleus accumbens?

Robert Correct. And that's enough to get the brain to keep doing the behaviour. However, nicotine and other drugs, like cocaine, can also create pleasurable feelings. Some more than others.

Jamie What's going on there?

Robert This is where we come to the shell. Cocaine releases dopamine in both the core *and* the shell. Dopamine release in the shell is linked to feelings of pleasure or even euphoria.

Jamie Aha! Thus creating a system where you have something that is pleasurable *and* addictive!

Robert Yes, and dopamine release in healthy behaviours is all well and good. For example, eating a healthy bowl of pasta creates a pleasurable experience which creates an impulse to repeat the behaviour. But because pleasure is driving the experience, if the activity stops being pleasurable – for example, if we've eaten too much pasta – the brain tells us to stop eating.

Jamie My brain doesn't always send me that message if it's macaroni cheese, but I get the point!

Robert (*laughs*) The brain can also weigh up prospects of different experiences and make decisions – here, that might be considering whether another helping of pasta is a good idea. It may not always arrive at a sensible answer, but at least it can weigh up the competing priorities. Now, what is unhealthy is when experiences or drugs lead directly to dopamine release in the core, bypassing this adaptive process and creating an urge to engage in a behaviour whether or not it is pleasurable or healthy.

Jamie   And then we're at risk of falling into a downward spiral.

Robert   Interestingly, during a cocaine binge, the pleasure itself diminishes while the impulse to do the behaviour increases.

Jamie   It's quite an unpleasant thought that there are activities that keep us locked into such un-enjoyable cycles.

Robert   That's why learning about the mechanisms in the brain can help us to combat these influences more effectively.

Jamie   Every so often, I'll try to go on a news blackout where I'll avoid all the websites I'd normally visit. And then I'll catch myself typing in the address of a news website unconsciously. Before I know it, I'm back looking at the news again! Reward without pleasure.

Robert   In fact, as we've said, the news is often very punishing. It makes us feel bad.

Jamie   But there are also excellent and important articles out there, which means it's unpredictably and intermittently rewarding, and that makes reading the news even more addictive.

Robert   Pretty clever stuff. But in the same way that we may try and avoid 'empty calories' when we're eating, we may want to try and avoid 'empty rewards' of this kind.

Jamie And that's just the news! Gambling companies must be having a golden time now with all the betting apps on our phones.

Robert The people who make these apps may not know the exact science behind how the brain works, but they certainly know how to take advantage of our brain's weaknesses.

Jamie It seems that in order to live a happier life, I should be replacing activities that are rewarding but not enjoyable with activities that are rewarding *and* enjoyable.

Robert I agree. Although, of course, there will be challenges. We need to recognise that, because of the way our brain works, our job is never done. By which I mean our animal brain will always try to take us back to our phone needlessly. And it's made especially difficult because most people need to use their phones for work or to stay in contact with people.

Jamie So, we might pick up our phone with the intention of sending an email and end up down a YouTube rabbit hole for hours. We've been stealthily hijacked.

Robert Yes. It's a bit like eating fast-food burgers one after the other without even thinking about it. That's where we need the human brain to step in and make changes.

Jamie I've heard some people criticise the 'younger generation' and say they're only interested in 'instant gratification'. Is part of that criticism founded in the way these phones work on our animal brains?

Robert I would be wary of dismissing a whole generation that way. I was in the cinema recently and a man who was about my age couldn't stop checking his phone – he took it out every ten minutes. It was incredibly annoying.

Jamie Tell me about it!

Robert It may be that teenagers are using social media more and, therefore, are more subject to the tricks that are used to keep people on their phones. But it's certainly no inherent fault.

Jamie I feel this discussion could also be useful in helping to understand some other behaviour that we see on social media. I'm thinking about people who 'troll' online – winding other people up, abusing or harassing them, and generally being antagonistic. A lot of times, I get the sense that the trolls simply want a reaction. And, sometimes, they seem to get into genuinely heated debates with the people they are unfairly antagonising. And I've always thought: they must be carrying a lot of negative emotions. Of course, they may also feel a sense of power and gratification, but it can often seem like the exchanges provoke actual anger in the troll!

Robert It's an interesting observation, and very possible. The behaviour is rewarding irrespective of whether it's enjoyable or not.

Jamie I think it applies to some news commentators or 'shock-jocks' who say cruel and provocative things as well. They seem to be rewarded by getting a reaction but are actually quite angry by the reaction they've provoked, too.

Robert Which is ironic because their behaviour is designed to create a hostile reaction. But the behaviour gets rewarded and goes round and round in a cycle of outrage.

Jamie So, it's possible that we're often caught in this loop of rewarding behaviour which hardly anybody is actually enjoying!

Robert Yes, it's a cruel quirk of the brain that has been successfully exploited by social media and various news websites.

Jamie What can we do about it?

Robert The answer is going to seem obvious: you stop rewarding the behaviour. You simply do not react to people whose behaviour you don't want to encourage.

Jamie Never?

Robert *Non-reward* is a very important process for extinguishing a behaviour. But – and it's a big but – if you're going to use non-reward to extinguish the behaviour, you've got to do it all the time. The worst thing you can do is to use non-reward most of the time, and then, every now and then, give in and react. That will make the behaviour even stronger because of the variable-ratio schedule of reinforcement we discussed earlier.

Jamie Wow. So, the advice to block people on Twitter, for example, is probably correct.

Robert Even blocking them gives a reaction. But it may work. Twitter currently has a mute option, although these websites are changing features fairly regularly. Ideally, the website itself would offer you a way of muting or blocking someone without them knowing about it so there's no reaction and no reward for them.

Jamie It sounds as though our animal brain is very fallible.

Robert But also utterly ingenious.

Jamie Now you've pointed it out, the difference between reward and enjoyment appears obvious. And it seems absolutely critical to understanding what's going on inside our brains in the 21st century.

KEY POINTS

- In psychology, the term *'reward'* describes an event that motivates a person or animal to repeat a given behaviour.

- Rewards are not always enjoyable. The brain can tell you to repeat a behaviour even if that behaviour isn't fun – for example, mindlessly scrolling through a news website.

- A part of the brain called the *nucleus accumbens* plays an important role in processing rewards.

- Dopamine release in the *core* of the nucleus accumbens creates the *impulse* to repeat a behaviour in a given situation. Dopamine release in the *shell* makes you *want* to repeat a behaviour to make you feel good.

- Where possible, focus on activities you find both rewarding *and* enjoyable.

- If you want to extinguish a behaviour, stop rewarding it entirely.

10. Habituation And Sensitisation

Jamie So, we've talked about how rewards and pleasure don't always go together. What about activities that are enjoyable for a while but then get boring? Like watching someone juggle ...

Robert (*laughs*) No offence to jugglers! Well, there's a form of learning I mentioned earlier which is, rather confusingly, called *habituation.*

Jamie From that, I'm guessing habituation has nothing to do with habits ...

Robert You're guessing right. Habituation is a form of learning in which a stimulus provokes less and less of a reaction each time it occurs or the longer it goes on.

Jamie One of my friends had a child about a year ago and she was describing how excited her daughter was noticing trees for the first time. And I thought, it takes me a bit of effort to appreciate trees these days. I'm used to them now.

Robert Yes, we habituate to lots of things. It evolved to allow us to enjoy a balanced approach to threats and opportunities and not get single-mindedly fixated on one thing. For example, things that scare us initially can come to feel normal – like swimming in the ocean. And, of course, it stops us spending all day just staring open-mouthed at the sky!

Jamie Steve Martin has a great bit on this. He said the first time a limo comes to pick you up, you go, 'Wow, a *limo!*' The next day you walk outside and say, 'Where's the limo?'.

Robert And, as we discussed earlier, it happens with some drugs too. Users have to increase their dose to get the effect they're looking for.

Jamie Is there an opposite of habituation?

Robert Yes, it's called *sensitisation*. That's where we react more strongly each time something occurs. Imagine you're trying to get to sleep at night, but outside your window a dog starts barking. It might be a bit annoying at first, but if the dog continues throughout the night, it could become more and more irritating.

Jamie It would for me. So, let me get this straight, there are some things that our animal brain gets used to and other things that it reacts to increasingly strongly – habituation and sensitisation.

Robert And there are situations in which both of these things happen at the same time. As we said earlier, this includes stimulant drugs like cocaine. The more you take it, the less you enjoy it. But the urge to take the drug gets stronger and stronger.

Jamie And this is because the dopamine being released in the core is increasing while the dopamine released in the shell is decreasing.

Robert You've got it! Now, I'd like to take a brief diversion to talk about preferences – the things we like and why we like them.

Jamie My interest is duly piqued.

Robert A psychologist called Robert Zajonc did an interesting experiment where he showed participants a series of faces and asked them to rate how attractive the faces were. However, at some point during this long sequence, he started to show the same faces again. And he also asked the participants whether they thought they'd seen the faces before.

Jamie Which would be hard to remember after having seen so many?

Robert Indeed. And what Zajonc found was that people liked the faces more if they'd seen them before, even if they didn't remember previously seeing them!

Jamie They unconsciously felt better about the faces that were familiar.

Robert Precisely. In this case, contrary to the popular maxim, familiarity didn't breed contempt – it bred liking.

Jamie 'Familiarity breeds liking.' It's not as catchy.

Robert And, broadening out, this happens with other stimuli, too – such as food.

Jamie I remember we once had a heated discussion about this, and I was adamant that you couldn't shape people's tastes this way. And then you reminded me how I used to feel about tomatoes.

Robert You hated them as a child, but we kept putting them on your plate.

Jamie And now I quite like them.

Robert This an important principle when trying to get children to eat foods that are good for them but which they don't like. If you can find ways to encourage them to keep trying new foods, they will eventually come to like them.

Jamie But that's not always true. Some people never learn to like certain types of food.

Robert Yes. And this brings us back to habituation and sensitisation – some people become sensitised to what they experience as the *unpleasant* taste of, say, Brussels sprouts.

Jamie Like me.

Robert And I'm the opposite. I'm sensitised to the *pleasant* taste of them.

Jamie Clearly, your taste buds are defective. But you're saying you can sensitise to pleasant and unpleasant things. Is the same true with habituation?

Robert Generally speaking, emotional responses that depend on fear or novelty will tend to habituate over time. Hence our desire to chase the 'new'. The first time I saw a video in Ultra HD, it was pretty staggering. Now, I'm used to it.

Jamie So, although it's still impressive, your emotional response is less pronounced.

Robert Yes. That said, emotional responses that rely on improved understanding and recognition will sensitise over time.

Jamie Like with music? The first time you hear a song isn't usually the most enjoyable. As you get to know the melody and arrangement, you begin to get more and more out of it. You wait for your favourite moments.

Robert Until it starts to habituate and then it doesn't interest you so much anymore.

Jamie It's like our bodies are always pulling between habituation and sensitisation, subtly changing what we like and don't like. So, habituation explains why we don't just keep doing the same thing over and over again, even though it might be a lot of fun at first.

Robert That's one reason – another is *satiation*. Satiation is when I give you an ice cream, then another ice cream, then another one, and eventually you go, 'That's enough ice cream, thanks.'

Jamie Another form of learning?

Robert It's more of a physiological response when drive states are reduced. You're hungry, you eat, and eventually you become satiated. You don't want to eat any more, and if you did keep going, the feeling would actually become unpleasant.

Jamie Of course, many of us do overeat – especially with ultra-processed foods on the table. But I think everyone is familiar with feeling satiated.

Robert And it doesn't just apply to food. It can apply to drinking, sex, playing games, or even just having a conversation. That feeling of 'having had your fill'.

Jamie Let's go back to habituation for a moment. What can we do when people have become habituated to our efforts to influence them?

Robert Good question. Let's say you're working on a public health commercial to encourage people to quit smoking. You want to maximise the sustained impact within the budget you have.

Jamie Okay.

Robert When pictures of diseased lungs were first put on cigarette packets, it had some effect. But, over time, people became habituated and just got used to seeing these images.

Jamie So, a new approach was needed?

Robert Yes. And in the case of cigarettes, they decided to put them in plain packaging.

Jamie Which takes away a lot of the allure. The packets used to look so sophisticated and seductive! I never smoked, but I did like the branding.

Robert The old packaging made smoking seem exciting whereas the plain packaging doesn't use images or enticing fonts, so it doesn't interest the animal brain in that way.

Jamie But hang on – why didn't they just make the images more and more shocking?

Robert One way to overcome habituation *is* to make the stimulus more extreme. But there comes a point where that stops working, and then you need to revamp. Repetition, sensitisation, habituation and revamp is an important cycle that plays out in marketing and, indeed, entertainment.

Jamie   So, say you start a new ad campaign with a cute, funny dog as your mascot. As the adverts are repeated, maybe with slight variations, people come to like the dog and the adverts more and more – this is the sensitisation phase. Then the appeal starts to wane and it's not so charming or funny anymore, which is the habituation stage. Then you need to revamp it – so maybe the dog gets a new outfit or meets a rival cat mascot?

Robert   And then the cycle goes round again.

Jamie   Aha . . . then after a certain amount of time has passed, you can come back to the old idea but with a new twist.

Robert   Exactly right. That's why you see so many reboots, remakes and sequels in the cinema. They have the familiarity, which people like, but with a new edge that will appeal to the audience and give them an emotional hit.

Jamie   Superhero films have dominated cinema for some time now – people really love them. I have to confess, though, I don't usually get that excited by them. But you're saying that they tap into this cycle of repetition, sensitisation, habituation and revamp.

Robert   Right. And, obviously, if you're investing hundreds of millions of dollars, you probably won't want to bet it all on a brand-new concept that might not even work.

Jamie Studio executives will be nodding along, no doubt.

Robert We all cling to familiarity sometimes. When I was a child, I used to go to Madrid in Spain to visit my father. I'd go to the record store there and flick through the albums, and if I saw a band I was familiar with, I'd get a bit of a thrill. Even if they weren't a band I particularly followed. Familiarity in an unfamiliar environment can be very comforting.

Jamie I'd be remiss if I didn't put forward the view that, given our underlying psychology, the courage to try new things is to be doubly applauded.

Robert Very much so. Risk taking is at the heart of creativity and originality.

Jamie I tell you what, though – when something original is a success, it's very hard to follow up on.

Robert This is down to *adaptation*. After you've had a success, people come to expect your next venture to be amazing rather than 'quite good'. It explains why follow-up films, shows or books often fail to satisfy. Our expectations of them are through the roof because we've adapted to what came before.

Jamie I hate to admit it, but when someone recommends something very strongly to me, I can sometimes push against it. I go into the experience almost looking for flaws.

Robert I know what you mean. You go in thinking, 'Is this really as good as everyone says?'. It's a more critical and closed state to be in – which means you're likely to find more flaws – but it's a perfectly common thing.

Jamie Is there any way we can combat this?

Robert At a very personal level, you can avoid overselling a recommendation to someone as it might actually undermine their enjoyment of it.

Jamie Don't overhype to friends.

Robert And if you're somebody who's *creating* a follow-up experience – it might not be something artistic, it could be a guest's second visit to your hotel – I would recommend trying to leave room for a pleasant surprise. Five-star hotels work really hard to do this. It doesn't have to be a massive surprise – it might just be remembering what kind of shampoo a guest prefers. But these little surprises help create a positive overall impression and avoid the potentially negative effects of adaptation.

Jamie I get the sense that this knowledge is not only useful in understanding our animal brains, our emotional responses to things and how they fluctuate – but also in designing experiences for other people. It feels like it could be so easy to shift the blame onto customers or audiences for being too demanding. But actually, these processes are taking place in all of us, and they give us clues to what's going on with other people and *their* animal brains.

KEY POINTS

- *Habituation* is a form of learning in which a stimulus provokes less of a reaction each time we experience it.

- *Sensitisation* is a form of learning in which a stimulus provokes more of a reaction each time we experience it.

- *Satiation* is a physiological response when drive states are reduced, resulting in us feeling 'full'.

- Familiarity tends to breed liking.

- As our *adaptation* levels increase we can be harder to please.

- *Repetition, sensitisation, habituation and revamp* is a cycle that plays out clearly in the fields of marketing and entertainment.

11. Testosterone And Punishment

Robert I want to talk briefly about a hormone that has quite a drastic effect on the animal brain: testosterone.

Jamie Interesting! Am I right in thinking it's not only men who have testosterone?

Robert Correct. Everyone has a certain amount of testosterone, but, as teenagers reach puberty, males generally produce a lot more of it in the testes.

Jamie Is this why teenage boys can sometimes be a bit terrifying?

Robert Well, testosterone can be dangerous stuff but it's not a 'bad' hormone, per se. It's needed to build muscle and bone and it helps produce sperm. However, it has an interesting relationship with learning and punishment.

Jamie How so?

Robert Testosterone can make you *less able* to learn from punishment. So, when someone with high levels of testosterone accidentally crashes their motorbike, testosterone's job is to stop them learning from their mistakes.

Jamie I'm sorry – what?

Robert Think about it from an evolutionary point of view. Let's say you're a young male way back in hunter-gatherer times – your role is to go out and hunt and fight to protect your tribe. And even if you get hurt one day, you'll probably have to go out and do it all again the next day.

Jamie I don't think I'd have survived very long…

Robert Me neither. But you can see why testosterone would be beneficial. And if you think about how it plays out across human society, men tend to get involved with more violent crime, and more crime that is linked to behaving in dangerous ways.

Jamie So, testosterone encourages more risk-taking behaviour.

Robert And it fuels aggression as well as increasing sex-drive.

Jamie What a combination.

Robert Remember, it's important and natural for humans to have a strong desire to procreate. It's one of the reasons the species has survived! So, we need to think about making the most of testosterone – creating social structures that take advantage of it.

Jamie It makes me think of a routine Jerry Seinfeld did on helmets. Essentially, he says that helmets are a weird invention. Why did we invent them? Because we were doing activities that were cracking our skulls. But instead of stopping those activities . . . we made helmets.

Robert (*laughs*) The thing is, the animal brain – which is driven by testosterone – is going to do something dangerous. So, the human brain says, 'I can't stop you, but I can give you a helmet.' And now you can go rock-climbing, horse-riding, roller-blading etc.

Jamie I'm scared of heights, and I often think if everyone was like me, no buildings over ten feet tall would ever have been built.

Robert The risk-taking element of our animal brains has been hugely beneficial in many ways, as well as obviously being harmful in others. Think of planes and the risks involved in developing safe air-travel. There's a part of our nature which is quite willing to put ourselves in mortal danger because of its thirst for knowledge or status, amongst other things.

Jamie So, this is kind of an argument for health and safety procedures?

Robert As long as they're not too restrictive, yes. Health and safety procedures have been a huge advance in modern society that has meant fewer people die needlessly.

Jamie Going back to testosterone, does anything trigger it?

Robert As I say, it's always present at some level, although more in men than women. There's also more of it in people who are competitive, aggressive and risk-takers. In men, it appears to be increased by the presence of an attractive woman and by stimuli associated with competition and aggression – for example, handling a gun.

Jamie How else can we make the best of testosterone? Competitive sport springs to mind.

Robert Yes. Sport is partly a displacement activity for all those raging hormones, and it helps express them in a healthier way.

Jamie Just to be clear, you're not saying that whoever has the most testosterone is going to be the best at sport?

Robert No. Clearly in some sports, men will tend to have an advantage if the sport is dependent on physical strength – particularly at a professional level. But there are a lot of other factors involved.

Jamie And, of course, sport is good for us in so many ways – both for our physical and mental well-being. But can we go back for a moment to this bombshell that testosterone suppresses our ability to learn from punishment?

Robert We can. I used to know a young man who was constantly getting into trouble with the police. He'd get driving tickets for speeding or parking illegally and get points on his licence. But when he talked about it, he'd either blame other people or put it down to bad luck. The important lesson here, which we discussed in *Energise*, is worth repeating: when you're dealing with someone like this, punishing them may make you feel better, but it is unlikely to actually change their behaviour.

Jamie So, apart from putting safety precautions in the environment like speed bumps or cameras, what can we do?

Robert You can deal with the person when they're not in the thrall of testosterone. In other words, when they're calm. Although when those hormones kick in and you add in peer pressure, it's a tricky thing to control. But it's not always impossible. Yet again, it's about planning for occasions when our emotions are likely to be pushing us in unhealthy directions. You just have to remember that the person's learning mechanism is impaired when testosterone kicks in.

Jamie   I imagine there are other reasons why anti-social or destructive behaviour continues?

Robert Plenty, and we'll look at it in the context of addiction in the coming chapters. But one reason for this behaviour is that a person might expect to be punished for behaving badly but then isn't.

Jamie   So you think you'll be punished for . . . let's say, running a red light late at night, but then actually nothing happens.

Robert Correct. And if you don't get punished, the brain is positively rewarded, which means the behaviour can then become habitual. It's like the brain is testing the boundaries of what it can get away with.

Jamie   One often reads stories about an employee who works at a company and starts stealing small amounts of money but doesn't get caught, so they start taking more and more.

Robert Another interesting example is when you accidentally get away with something. Imagine walking out of a supermarket and then realising you'd forgotten to scan the bunch of bananas you'd hung on the front of your trolley. Your animal brain is thinking, 'Hey, I got away with that. Maybe I'll do that deliberately next time.'

Jamie   Sneaky.

Robert As a side-note, the opposite happens when you expect a reward but no reward arrives. So, if it was your birthday and you were expecting a present but you didn't get anything – that would feel like a punishment.

Jamie Sounds like my last birthday!

Robert Now, now. I got you something . . . in the end. But the main point of this chapter is simply to give an understanding of how testosterone can actively stop the brain from learning and encourage risk-taking behaviour. In a way, it's to be expected, particularly in young men. So, instead of railing against it, you can anticipate it and deal with it accordingly.

KEY POINTS

- *Testosterone* is a hormone that is produced by all humans, although generally males produce more than females.

- Testosterone is needed to help build muscle, bone and produce sperm. It encourages more risk-taking behaviour and increases aggression and sex-drive.

- Testosterone reduces our ability to learn from punishment.

- Testosterone can be very helpful when harnessed – for example, in sports, for procreation, or self-protection.

- Health and safety rules can be useful in reducing the negative consequences of testosterone.

- It is easier to counsel someone when they're calm and not overwhelmed by testosterone.

12. Addiction

Jamie We're finally here! It's your Mastermind specialist subject: addiction. From what we've discussed, this looks like an area where the animal brain can really go wrong.

Robert Yes, and the first thing to note is that there is a lot of misunderstanding about the nature of addiction.

Jamie How so?

Robert Let's look again at drug addiction. The standard idea runs something like this: you start taking a drug – maybe it's for pleasure, to get high, out of curiosity or because of peer pressure. But the more you do it, the more your body gets used to the drug. So, if you're trying to get high, you have to increase the dose to get the effect you're looking for. And the more your body gets used to the drug, the more it can't function properly without it. If you try to stop using the drug, you start to experience *withdrawal symptoms*, which are very unpleasant and can even be life threatening. Eventually, you end up taking the drug to stave off the withdrawal symptoms. Instead of taking the drug because you want to, you are taking it because you need to.

Jamie Wait – you're saying that's *not* what happens? Didn't you tell me earlier that's exactly what happens?!

Robert What I'm saying is that it's not the whole story. If drug addiction were just about that, curing people of their addiction would be a fairly simple matter. We would just need to get them into hospital and look after them until the withdrawal symptoms subsided, and the job would be done. In fact, almost everyone who goes through this kind of 'detox' treatment relapses back to drugs afterwards – usually sooner rather than later.

Jamie So, what role do withdrawal symptoms play? Surely, they must be contributing to relapses?

Robert Yes – there are things like delirium tremens, which can occur during alcohol withdrawal. Delirium tremens can involve deeply unpleasant symptoms like confusion, shaking hands or feet and hallucinations.

Jamie I've seen those dramatised in films and TV shows – just watching a brief montage of an actor *pretending* to go through that is unpleasant.

Robert I don't want to imply that withdrawal symptoms play no role in addiction, but the point I'm making is that in order to understand addiction, we have to figure out what's causing the addict to feel such a strong need or urge. Only by doing that can we help them recover.

Jamie So, it's not just a case of getting over *physical* withdrawal symptoms – there are other things going on. Is it true that the more severe the symptoms are, the harder it is to give up the drug?

Robert Well, studies have found that in people addicted to heroin, the severity of the withdrawal symptoms does not predict whether or not they will relapse.

Jamie That appears to close the door on that theory.

Robert In fact, many people who are addicted to stimulant drugs, such as cocaine, don't actually experience withdrawal symptoms.

Jamie If their body doesn't need it in order to function, why don't they just stop?

Robert As it happens, most people who are addicted to drugs that produce feelings of euphoria continue getting a positive experience. In other words, they still get high after decades of use.

Jamie Even if it's causing serious problems in other areas of their lives?

Robert I'm afraid so.

Jamie So, how *should* we be thinking about addiction and the animal brain?

Robert Think about this: what do addictive behaviours have in common?

Jamie I guess they all involve people behaving in ways that are damaging to themselves and others, and it's very hard for them to stop.

Robert That's right, but let's expand on that. They all involve people feeling an *abnormally strong need or urge* to repeatedly engage in a behaviour *for a variety of reasons* despite the prospect of serious harm to themselves or others. This need or urge develops with repeated experience of the behaviour – sometimes quickly and sometimes over quite a long period of time.

Jamie Aha – that's a much more thorough and useful definition. But is addiction a disease, as many people claim?

Robert It's better to think of it as a disorder. The word 'disease' carries with it the baggage of infection or some very obvious brain pathology. It's reasonable to think of addiction as 'abnormal', but we cannot be sure that in every case there is some obvious brain pathology you could point to.

Jamie How do you mean?

Robert Well, the addiction may turn out to be a 'normal' human response to an 'abnormal' situation. The classic example is US soldiers in Vietnam in the 1970s. Large numbers of them showed every sign of being addicted to opiates. It was expected that when they returned to the US after the war was over, there would be a huge need for treatment services to deal with the problem.

Jamie But that didn't happen?

Robert No. To most people's surprise, veterans returning to the US seemed to instantly 'recover' from their opiate addiction. The pattern of drug use was a response to the appalling situation they faced in Vietnam, together with an abundant supply of drugs and drug use being common amongst the soldiers.

Jamie It was the situation that was 'abnormal', not their brains.

Robert To a large extent, yes. But, of course, many soldiers didn't become addicted to opiates. There must have been something about the ones who did that made them vulnerable. So, the addiction, in fact, arose from a combination of their vulnerability, their situation, and the effects of the drug itself.

Jamie So, some people may be more vulnerable to becoming addicts than others?

Robert Good question. Let's take another example: addiction to alcohol. In countries like the UK and US, about ten percent of people who drink alcohol can be classed as being addicted. And there are many more who struggle to regulate their alcohol intake – it's a very common problem.

Jamie One in ten – that's surprising.

Robert I know. For some, the addiction can be so powerful that it ruins their lives and the lives of those around them.

Jamie And these people who get addicted are especially vulnerable?

Robert Yes. People who become addicted to alcohol are very likely to have previously suffered from psychological problems, whether it be anxiety, depression or some form of impulse control disorder. They are more likely than other people to have suffered abuse as children. And they are more likely to have grown up with one or both parents addicted to alcohol. There's also a strong genetic link with addiction to alcohol which has been shown by studies of twins reared together versus reared apart.

Jamie I remember reading that someone had asked the famous hell-raising actor Peter O'Toole why he drank, and he'd simply said, 'Pain'. Is alcohol a way of numbing or 'medicating' difficult feelings?

Robert In some cases, yes – but not always. For these vulnerable people, alcohol just hits the spot in terms of the reward pathways in the animal brain we talked about earlier. And, as I say, there's a strong genetic basis for this.

Jamie Alcohol is obviously widely available to buy in shops and bars, and I can see how a vulnerable person might become addicted to it. But what about harder, recreational drugs like cocaine?

Robert Let's zoom out for a moment and imagine the culture in which someone might take cocaine. Why would someone take it in the first place? It's got to be appealing in some way. And it will only be appealing to people who are curious and not too bothered about doing things that are frowned upon or illegal. That will generally be sensation seekers and not the kind of people who think they need to follow the rules.

Jamie I imagine in some cases, with peer pressure, drug-taking can also be rewarded by the people around you.

Robert Very much so. You've got to be in an environment where the opportunity arises – often amongst family or friends. And that opportunity creates a vulnerability because if you don't have the opportunity to take a drug, obviously you can't get addicted to it. So, right at the beginning, you have all these social and psychological factors coming into play.

Jamie Drug-taking doesn't exist in a vacuum.

Robert Correct. So, now you're in a situation where some cocaine is going round at a party, and someone offers you a 'line'.

Jamie Tom Waits, the musician, has a song with the refrain: 'The first one's always free'.

Robert Very often, it is. Let's say you decide to snort it... Now, you're in a different ballpark. Previously, the drug appealed to you based on social and psychological factors. It was all about appeal. Now it's about biological reward. And when you get rewarded, your brain wants to do whatever you just did again. Only in this case, the reward isn't a tasty meal or a pay check. The drug has short-circuited all of that and tells you, 'Just take that drug again!'

Jamie By releasing dopamine in the core of the nucleus accumbens! So you feel a strong urge to take it whether you enjoy it or not.

Robert And whether people are peer pressuring you or not.

Jamie 'Just take the drug.' Then what happens?

Robert You take it again. Then the dopamine system in your brain begins to adapt and learn. The drug is now driving your animal brain. But you're not just an animal, you're also a human. So, as a human you've got to make sense of it.

Jamie You tell yourself a story, create a narrative.

Robert Exactly. Your human brain says, 'Why am I taking this drug?' And it may actually go into denial, rationalising and minimising the consequences.

Jamie 'I only take it on the weekends' or 'It's just a social thing'.

Robert Or it may come up with a solution along the lines of, 'This is who I am.' Your *identity* becomes that of someone who takes cocaine.

Jamie And once your identity changes, other things follow too?

Robert Indeed. Over time, you may start to change your circle of friends or get into trouble with the law etc. And you'll start to create beliefs about society and what the drug is doing for you – for example, you may begin to believe that it helps you in particular ways. Perhaps you think it helps you function more effectively, helping you socialise or work longer hours.

Jamie I've noticed that people who do recreational drugs often want you to try them as well. Or they get quite angry that the government has made them illegal.

Robert That's right. What started out as a reward in a little part of the brain – the nucleus accumbens – has now expanded into other parts of the brain. And then, perhaps, you start dealing a bit on the side and earning money, and you think, 'This is what I do.' It becomes an even bigger part of your identity. And that little acorn – taking your first line of cocaine – has grown into a fully-fledged tree of addiction.

Jamie Poetically phrased but also terrifying.

Robert And then, perhaps, you try different drugs – maybe some sedatives to counter the effects of the cocaine. So, you become a 'poly-drug user'. In other words, you regularly take more than one drug.

Jamie And you're just getting in deeper and deeper.

Robert As I say, people who get into real difficulties with alcohol or illicit drugs are very often in serious distress as a result of their upbringing and mental health problems.

Jamie That's very sad.

Robert It's important to recognise that drugs can *feel* as though they offer a temporary relief from the hell of someone's life. But the reality is they come with a massive cost that is incredibly destructive. And one of the things people who offer drug treatment services will tell you is that they're not just dealing with addiction, they're also trying to help the person put together some kind of life that will give them real satisfaction and purpose.

Jamie Very interesting. I feel I have a much more three-dimensional understanding of what addiction is now.

Robert As always, it's about broadening *and* sharpening our understanding – seeing how the different pieces fit together.

Jamie So, we've looked at alcohol and cocaine. I'm wondering about other addictions: social media, gaming, smoking. Are we going to get into those?

Robert Your wish is my command . . .

KEY POINTS

- *Addiction* is a disorder that involves a person feeling an abnormally strong need or urge to repeatedly engage in a behaviour for a variety of reasons despite the prospect of serious harm to themselves or others.

- Dealing with drug addiction is more complicated than just managing *withdrawal symptoms* – although withdrawal symptoms may play a role.

- Many people who become addicts are vulnerable in some way. They may have suffered physical, sexual or mental abuse or have a range of mental health difficulties.

- People who take illegal drugs tend to care less about behaving in ways that are frowned upon by wider society.

- An individual's likelihood of becoming addicted to alcohol is, to quite a large degree, inherited from their parents.

- Drug-taking doesn't exist in a vacuum. It starts in an environment where the opportunity arises, usually amongst friends or family.

- Drug-taking can become part of a person's identity. Their human brain may construct stories about why taking drugs is important to them.

13. Other Addictions

Jamie You're well-known for your work on cigarette addiction. Indeed, we wrote a book together a few years back called *The Smoke-Free Formula* for people trying to give up smoking.

Robert Available in all good online bookshops for less than the price of a packet of cigarettes!

Jamie (*laughs*) Perhaps we can talk about some of the features of cigarette addiction and what principles we can draw from it?

Robert Absolutely. If you remember earlier, we talked about primary and secondary reinforcers. With smoking, nicotine is a primary reinforcer that pretty much hacks our animal brain's reward system. And then there are things around it – like the packaging, for example – that act as secondary reinforcers.

Jamie So, even though some of the secondary reinforcers can be relatively arbitrary – say, the type of cardboard the packaging is made from – they become associated with the reward of inhaling nicotine through the cigarette?

Robert That's right. Now, think about how someone starts smoking. They may simply be offered a cigarette by a friend, and they don't know what brand it is or how strong it is – they just take a few puffs. However, before long, they'll begin buying their own cigarettes. And they may try a few different brands, but eventually they'll settle on just one or two.

Jamie   And these brands become part of their identity.

Robert   Yes. And this process in addiction is what's known as *narrowing of a repertoire*. So, now, it's not just the nicotine hit that is part of the addiction package, it's the nicotine plus the secondary reinforcers. And the smoker becomes more and more conditioned to the exact sensory properties of this package, which is very powerfully reinforcing.

Jamie   You're saying they're not just addicted to cigarettes, they're addicted to the specific type of cigarette.

Robert   Yes – which is why switching brands can be surprisingly unappealing for many smokers. If you take away these secondary reinforcers, smokers find it uncomfortable.

Jamie   So, this must be true for other types of addiction, too?

Robert   Very much so – alcoholics often have a 'drink of choice'. Technically, they could drink a whole range of alcoholic beverages, but they tend to narrow their repertoire to one or two specific drinks – perhaps cider, whiskey or white wine.

Jamie   Earlier, we said that a rat could be motivated to press a lever 30 times for food if secondary reinforcers – like flashing lights – were used. So, here, the addictive behaviours are strengthened by secondary reinforcers like packaging and branding.

Robert Generally speaking, yes. I'm over-simplifying a bit, but you can also see this with computer games. When people get hooked on these, they tend to go for just one or two specific games.

Jamie I have a few friends who say they're 'addicted' to gaming, and you're right – it's often just one game they love to play!

Robert And gaming can be lots of fun and not necessarily unhealthy. But there are people who do end up spending more time and money than is good for them playing games. I would prefer to call that a 'para-addiction'.

Jamie So, it's 'like' an addiction?

Robert But not as compulsive or harmful, and more driven by *wanting* than *needing*.

Jamie It's more about pursuing a pleasant experience.

Robert Correct. People who get really into a particular computer game also tend to really enjoy it. The strength of their desire to play the game roughly matches the enjoyment they get out of it. With heroin or cigarette addiction, by contrast, the behaviour is being primarily driven by a feeling of need.

Jamie Would you say shopping could become a para-addiction?

Robert What I'm suggesting is that some people can experience a 'para-addiction' to shopping, food, computer games, and social media. Their behaviour can look obsessional and can certainly harm them, but, usually, not to the same degree as a full-blown addiction. I accept that it's a matter of judgement where one draws the line because these things are all a matter of degree, but I think it's a useful distinction.

Jamie Can para-addictions go on to become full addictions, then?

Robert Yes – although it's relatively uncommon.

Jamie I get the sense that para-addictions tend to be behaviours you're more likely to limit than get rid of entirely.

Robert Indeed. A lot of people find they want to use social media a bit but end up spending far more time on it than they want.

Jamie I had a strange experience recently on YouTube. I'd started a video series on how to write song lyrics. After posting the first few videos, I found the view count suddenly became very important to me. And every time you sign in, the site shows you statistics about how well your new video is 'performing' compared to your last video. Very quickly, I found myself compulsively checking it to see if I had new likes, subscribers or comments. And checking my statistics momentarily alleviated my anxiety, but it would emerge again minutes later, and I'd feel the need to check the site again.

Robert It sounds as though the platform is encouraging behaviours similar to those seen in people with obsessive compulsive disorder with the 'checking'. What did you do?

Jamie I spent some time thinking about the framework the website had given me – it had effortlessly linked the idea that the more views my video had, the more valuable it was. I had to consciously realise that the actual video didn't change whether five or 500 people saw it – what made it valuable, in my eyes, was the quality of the video itself.

Robert Very interesting point.

Jamie In practical terms, I decided to put some boundaries on my usage: I made a rule to only check my account twice a week and to log out after each time I used it.

Robert Putting a barrier between yourself and the automatic checking.

Jamie That's right. And it was hard for a week, but then I pretty much got used to it. And my mind was free from worrying about view counts and statistics. So, I focussed instead on the qualitative experience of making the videos rather than the numbers.

Robert I like what you've done there. These platforms include a whole package of rewards that include social approval but also other 'features' like notifications and comparative statistics.

Jamie I found it very corrupting, and I know many others do too.

Robert You rightly figured out that you'd need stronger behaviour change techniques than just saying to yourself, 'I'll try not to check'.

Jamie They appear to be working for me, but I was surprised by how quickly using the platform changed what I did and how I felt. Are there any other techniques you could suggest?

Robert *Behavioural substitution* would be one. So, similar to the way we talked about swapping in healthier habits earlier, you can make a plan to do something else when you feel like checking your social media accounts. It might be reading a book or putting on some music, for example.

Jamie So, you choose to spend that time doing something that is rewarding *and* enjoyable!

Robert You can also implement an 'IF-THEN Rule'. So, if you've got a problem with gaming for too long, you can set up a rule: IF you've been playing for 30 minutes, THEN you'll take a break for five minutes.

Jamie Makes sense.

Robert When it comes to a para-addiction, I would say it's important to ask yourself how much the behaviour is bothering you. The aim is to make your life better and give you a bit more control. So, ask what pattern of behaviour would suit your purposes best. How would you feel only using social media once a day or once a week or once a month?

Jamie And, at this stage, you're just taking an educated guess?

Robert Yes, and you might not be correct. But it gives you a starting point and allows you to set a clear behavioural goal which can be adjusted as you experiment with different strategies.

Jamie Then it's a case of trial and error?

Robert Indeed – be your own psychologist. Also, realising that a package of stimuli is particularly powerful can help you understand how to dismantle it.

Jamie How would you do that?

Robert Perhaps gaming gives you a social reward, but unfortunately it takes up a lot of time and leaves you feeling bad afterwards. You might be able to limit your gaming use and seek that social reward elsewhere – say, joining an evening class or sports club.

Jamie Separating out what you actually want from the activity and seeing if you can get it in a healthier way.

Robert A lot of us read the news because it gives us a feeling of connection with the outside world and current affairs. But do we need to read the news *every time* we pick up our phones? Is there another way to interact with the larger world? Again, we're trying to limit empty rewards and replace them with things that actually fulfil us.

Jamie Reflecting in this way can help us set new goals or generate more options. And then we can experiment to see what works for us.

Robert Exactly.

Jamie And people can also seek support from other sources.

Robert Absolutely. Sometimes, you need specific tools to deal with specific problems. For example, for people who want to reduce their alcohol intake, there's an app called 'Drink Less'. It has strategies and tips particularly related to cutting down alcohol consumption.

Jamie And there are also apps to help limit screen time and social media usage as well. Though it feels a bit ironic to *use* technology to help us *use less* technology!

Robert I know. Also, there are weight-loss groups and programmes for people wanting to change their diet or lifestyles. A lot of the same behavioural tools apply, but it can be extremely useful to get tailored support for the challenge you're struggling with.

Jamie There are lots of options.

Robert That's the takeaway. And I'll expand more on this in our next chapter where we'll look at recovery from serious addictions.

KEY POINTS

- Addictive behaviours respond to a package of primary and secondary reinforcers which strengthen the power of the addiction.

- *Narrowing of a repertoire* occurs when the addicted person becomes more and more attracted to the exact properties of the addictive behaviour – for example, an alcoholic having 'a drink of choice'.

- People often refer to behaviours such as overeating, using too much social-media and excessive shopping as 'addictions', but it's probably better to think of them as 'para-addictions' – they have some of the features of addiction but are not severe enough to qualify.

- Strategies for overcoming para-addictions include:
  o behavioural substitution i.e. doing something else instead.
  o making 'IF-THEN Rules' – for example, IF you've been playing a computer game for 30 minutes, THEN you'll take a 5 minute break.

- defining an ideal relationship with the activity and working to achieve that.
- using tailored apps or websites to help you monitor or shape your behaviour.
- joining support groups.
- figuring out what underlying positive experience the activity is offering you and meeting that need elsewhere.

14. Recovery From Addiction

Jamie I'm fascinated by these new ways – by which I mean, new to me – of looking at addiction. They seem to promise a variety of solutions. So, what can you tell us about recovery and overcoming addiction?

Robert Just as there are lots of routes into addiction, there are lots of routes out of it. And there is a lot of luck involved. Having conducted research into addiction for a number of decades now, and in particular into helping people stop smoking, the thing I always say to smokers who want to stop is: *keep trying*. Every quit attempt is another roll of the dice.

Jamie I've heard you say this before, but I worry it seems a bit random – like we don't really know what helps and so the person should just . . . keep trying things.

Robert We do know methods that help, but the problem is that, despite this, there are so many elements in play. So, luck still has an important role.

Jamie Elements in play? What do you mean? Can you give us a real-world example?

Robert Okay, let's talk about tobacco smokers – as opposed to cannabis smokers. Now, there are countless studies showing that if you rely on willpower alone when trying to quit smoking, the odds of making it to a year are about 1 in 36.

Jamie That sounds pretty low.

Robert It does, but now imagine you have two dice, and your job is to throw two sixes.

Jamie Okay . . .

Robert The chances of this happening are one in 36. But let's say you don't just get one attempt – you can keep trying! So, you throw again and again. And if you keep rolling the dice, the odds end up very much in your favour.

Jamie I see. So, after 10 or 20 unsuccessful attempts, you may feel as though you'll never be able to succeed, but the next time you try, you might well throw the two sixes and quit smoking.

Robert And that's just using willpower, alone. With smoking, you can stack the odds even more in your favour. Quite drastically, in fact. If you use a pill, such as varenicline (sold as Champix or Chantix) or bupropion (sold as Zyban), you can more than double the odds of success. And if you're lucky enough to have a specialist stop-smoking counsellor in your area, you can double the odds again. So, if you use varenicline and specialist support, it increases the odds to one in six.

Jamie That's a massive difference! I guess you still have to roll the dice and, who knows, maybe things don't work out that first go.

Robert Maybe not. But they're much more likely to work out after a few goes. The secret to stopping smoking is literally to *keep trying*. I would suggest trying once a year, at least. Each time you try, you should stack the odds in your favour by using treatments that have been found to be effective by clinical research.

Jamie I notice you used the plural there, 'treatments'. Other than varenicline and counselling, what else is out there?

Robert There are nicotine replacement therapies like skin patches, chewing gum, lozenges and electronic cigarettes. Each has its pros and cons, but all of them improve your odds of success when you try to stop smoking.

Jamie Can this information be applied to other addictive behaviours?

Robert I believe so, yes. But there is another complication. With addiction to illicit drugs and alcohol, you will remember that I talked about a vulnerability stemming from difficulties people are having with their mental health or life situation. By and large, recovery from the addiction is going to have to address that vulnerability – and that can be very difficult.

Jamie I don't suppose there's a secret weapon we can deploy?

Robert Well, one thing that seems to emerge a lot from the research is harnessing the power of identity.

Jamie Change your name, move to a secret location. That sort of thing?

Robert (*laughs*) Not quite. It's about becoming *the kind of person* who doesn't take the drug or do the behaviour. The behaviour is simply incompatible with your identity. Quite often, this can mean developing an identity as someone who helps other addicts to recover.

Jamie I can think of some celebrities who were addicted to substances who've since taken on this role – people like Elton John or Russell Brand.

Robert That's right. It helps you and, hopefully, you can help other people who are struggling with addiction. But there are other ways in which identities can change as well. It may be that you get married or have children or grandchildren, and you want to take care of yourself for their benefit.

Jamie Wanting to be healthy so you can be a good partner or play a better role as a parent.

Robert Those can be very strong motivations for some people.

Jamie But I imagine changing identity can be a daunting thing.

Robert Absolutely. Some people may have an instant epiphany, but mostly the transition will take time and perseverance. Which is one of the reasons why it's a good idea to seek support.

Jamie I've heard that seeking support is vital, but many people find it hard to ask for help.

Robert Yes, because it means openly admitting you have a problem. And that can mean you have to come to terms with your behaviour, which can feel uncomfortable and troubling. However, it's an important step.

Jamie What is this transition state like? Presumably you'll want to avoid tempting situations?

Robert It will depend on the drug or behaviour. But, say, if you were back at a party and someone offered you a line of coke, you may have to take a moment to consciously reflect on your plan to stay clean. So, you may think to yourself, 'I want to, but I'd better not.' And that may happen any number of times.

Jamie Why not just avoid going to the party?

Robert That's a good idea – especially early in the process – because it helps minimise your exposure to triggers. But at the same time, you'll have to accept that temptations and cravings will occur. So, you want to have a plan in place to deal with them. Which might be calling a friend or getting absorbed in a different activity. But each time you avoid engaging with the addiction, you train your animal brain to extinguish the behaviour. And that takes it out of what we can call the *behaviour repertoire*.

Jamie What's that?

Robert Well, you're a vegetarian, so eating meat is simply not in your behaviour repertoire. So, the reason 'the first one's always free' is because once a behaviour is in your menu of behaviours, if you will, you're much more likely to do it.

Jamie Hence, all the giveaways from soft drink companies when they launch a new flavour or product. We know, now, that our animal brain tends to like people who give us primary reinforcers, particularly for free, so it works doubly in the drink companies' favour. You know, it makes me think of an old teacher of mine, who was an ex-smoker. He said, 'The best way to stop smoking is never to start.'

Robert Right – don't even let it get into the behaviour repertoire.

Jamie I also remember going to a friend's flat when I was a teenager and someone bringing out a cigarette which was passed around the group one by one. And there was a lot of social pressure to try it. I was able to decline it at the time, but I do understand why people said yes. So, once it's in the behaviour repertoire, how do you get it out?

Robert The important point, which we mentioned earlier, is that you don't want to occasionally cave in.

Jamie Because that will actually strengthen the behaviour due to the variable-ratio schedule of reinforcement?

Robert Correct. That variable schedule is so powerful *because* it's intermittent. The rule we use to help people stop smoking is, 'Not a puff, no matter what.'

Jamie Surely one puff isn't going to kill you?

Robert The thing is, for an addict, it usually won't just be one puff. It will quickly become a whole pack.

Jamie I know you're saying that people mustn't have lapses in order to extinguish the behaviour, but people *do* have lapses!

Robert You're right, of course. But ultimately, in the addictions I'm talking about right now – i.e. not the para-addictions – you want to extinguish the behaviour entirely. So, I'm walking you through what an ideal quit attempt would be.

Jamie   And that's still possible after a number of faulty quit attempts?

Robert   Absolutely.

Jamie   I see. So, what is the key message you want our readers to take away?

Robert   The key message is that addiction develops because people come to experience a powerful need or urge relating to a drug or behaviour. This can happen for a wide variety of reasons. Whatever is causing this has to be addressed in both the short and long term for the person to 'recover'. This could involve a change of life circumstances, a sudden epiphany, a 'maturing out', an improvement in ability to handle mental health problems, drugs that reduce the cravings, to name a few. Very often, it's some combination of these. For many people, the vulnerability will still be there – either because it's innate, or deeply ingrained – so it's vital to continue to be vigilant about slipping back and to be ready to recommit to the change whenever needed.

Jamie   And I imagine to a lesser extent, some of these tools can apply to our para-addictions, too?

Robert   That's right. Keep trying. And if you relapse, don't become demoralised – spend some time reflecting on what went wrong and look to build on your previous experiences.

Jamie I think it's really encouraging that there are numerous paths out of addiction. And I also like the message that you have to keep rolling the dice in order to be successful. It can be so disheartening to try something once wholeheartedly and 'fail' – it's nice to know that persistence really can pay off.

Robert It definitely can!

KEY POINTS

- There are many routes out of addiction.

- The more times someone tries to overcome an addiction, the better their chances of success.

- Depending on the addiction, and by using the correct treatment, the odds of success can be drastically improved.

- If someone is using illicit drugs or is heavily into alcohol, the recovery will usually have to address the person's underlying vulnerability – i.e. their life circumstances, previous traumas etc.

- Identity can be a powerful tool for change. It can be beneficial for the person to view themselves as someone who 'doesn't take drugs' or 'helps others quit'.

- Every time someone trying to recover from drug-use successfully avoids engaging in the addiction, it trains the animal brain to extinguish the behaviour.

- It can be useful to minimise exposure to triggers – especially early in the recovery – but at the same time, it is important to accept that cravings will occur and plan ways to combat them.

15. Conclusion

Jamie I have to say, talking about this topic has really changed how I see the people around me. And it's made me a lot more conscious of our similarities to other animals. For example, I didn't realise how much we use touch in social situations.

Robert I've noticed that too. I suppose we've become hyper aware of touch and contact living through a global pandemic.

Jamie Watching the Tokyo Olympics, I noticed that as soon as athletes finished their event, they immediately hugged each other or their support staff. It doesn't strike me as a very 'human brain' thing to do. It seems tactile and more associated with bonding and soothing.

Robert Are there any other things you see differently now?

Jamie So many! First off, I'm amazed at how complex the animal brain is. How subtly it tunes into reward and punishment, and how the timing of the reward can impact on its learning. It's meant I've started to make a concerted effort to reward myself after I've done something positive. I hadn't fully realised how easy it was for me to punish myself after doing something good! And this new approach has transformed my relationship with writing – I really make sure to give myself praise and encouragement at the end of each session. Sometimes I even gee myself up while I'm writing, a bit like a runner mid-race clenching their fist and shouting, 'Come *on*!'.

Robert (*laughs*) That, I would like to see!

Jamie Similarly, I try to make sure I praise other people when they've done something I liked. I have to be honest and say that it doesn't always come naturally. For example, if I'm rehearsing with my band and someone comes up with a good part, I think I tend to have an unconscious attitude of, 'Assume what you're playing is good unless I tell you otherwise'. But I've noticed that this can leave band members feeling a little unsure of what to do because there's not really been any communication – so, sometimes they'll end up changing things I did actually like. Am I revealing too much here?!

Robert Not at all. I think there will be many other people who find it hard to remember to praise others. Anyway, you probably got that tendency from me in the first place!

Jamie I have to say the other absolute game-changer when it comes to timings of rewards was learning about the variable-ratio schedule of reinforcement – unpredictable intermittent rewards. You've been telling me about it since I was a kid, but it's only while working on this book that it's really hit home how powerful that reward schedule is. It can keep us doing a whole load of behaviours that are almost always punishing but occasionally rewarding. From small things like nagging, to big things like gambling.

Robert I would love to get the phrase 'variable-ratio schedule of reinforcement' into the vernacular.

Jamie (*laughs*) If 'supercalifragilisticexpialidocious' can, there's hope for you yet. And the concept is so worth knowing about.

Robert What else do you feel has stuck with you from delving into the animal brain?

Jamie Simple things like defining *wants* and *needs* clearly. Wants being an attraction towards an imagined positive future, and needs being a desire to get rid of an unpleasant feeling. All my life I've wanted to play music, but I have a need to play as well because if I don't play, I feel very bad. I think it's the same across different fields, too. Some actors talk about the need to act, and it has a real edge of desperation to it, as though they don't know who they are without it – or they're not 'whole' without it. I think the truth is they both want and need to act, but I suspect tuning into the want aspect will lead to a better, happier life.

Robert It's like two sides of a coin. And you're right – focussing on what you want rather than feeling compelled by what you need can lead to a more enjoyable engagement with the world.

Jamie Which leads me on to that distinction between reward and enjoyment. I'd never thought of it that way. There are a lot of activities, usually involving our phones, which are rewarding but not enjoyable. And then we get to the end of the day or week and realise we've wasted all our time. And even though we resolve to do better, we don't seem to have learned from it the next time we get sucked into phone-world. I really didn't understand why that was until we discussed how the animal brain works.

Robert It seems simple – do activities you find both rewarding and enjoyable. But it's not always straightforward.

Jamie And I was fascinated by our talks on building healthy habits. The very first point: define the habit you want to build as specifically as possible. I've found that very useful. It takes things away from vague, foggy notions like 'Just be healthier' or 'Exercise more'.

Robert When you define what you're trying to achieve in specific terms, it means you can make it much easier to perform the behaviour, measure it and find out what's working and what isn't.

Jamie I also often think about the idea of 'haphazard routines' and being prepared to do the habit at an unanticipated time. With a haphazard routine, somehow I feel I've already lost – I should have had a regular routine and now I'm basically screwed!

Robert Which, as you're intimating, is a totally counter-productive approach.

Jamie Now, I can accept there are times that I will have to work with a haphazard routine. And if I can recognise this, perhaps lower my expectations of what I can achieve slightly, I can still get good work done.

Robert This is all very encouraging to hear.

Jamie I always like it when you broaden out my sense of a concept – like you did with impulses and inhibitions. The idea that we always act based on whatever is the strongest impulse at any given time feels quite revolutionary.

Robert It's one of the maxims I love repeating.

Jamie I think it just explains behaviour so well. Have you ever been on the way to a party with someone and they've said they're not going to drink or smoke that night? But as soon as they arrive, it all seems to go out the window, and they spend the night drinking and smoking away!

Robert And often feel guilty the next morning.

Jamie It seems obvious to me now that the impulse to behave in those ways was just much stronger at the party. Talking them out of it in that moment would be like trying to talk a cat out of chasing a mouse.

Robert Hence, the need to plan with the human brain when the animal brain isn't so overwhelmed with those impulses.

Jamie It's so useful! And hearing your thoughts on the repetition, sensitisation, habituation and revamp cycle has also made me a bit more forgiving.

Robert Oh, really?

Jamie Well, I guess I've been frustrated at how cinema has changed – à la Martin Scorsese. But now I see that creating original work is doubly challenging given our intrinsic psychology. Our preference for the familiar with slight alterations can be overwhelming, particularly if studios are pumping big money into it and want a sure-fire return. Don't get me wrong, I haven't changed my stance on the value of original filmmaking, but I think I have a better sense of what we're up against, and I can recognise that these tendencies exist in all of us.

Robert And, of course, it's not always negative. It's nice to go to the same restaurant rather than having to find a new one each time.

Jamie Well, we always come back to this one near your house, don't we?

Robert Indeed. I thought our chapter on testosterone was pretty interesting.

Jamie It was! The other day a teenage boy riding a scooter sped past me on the pavement, and I thought about it. I was still annoyed, but the knowledge that testosterone increases risk-taking behaviour and means we learn less well from punishment allowed me some ironic distance.

Robert That's very enlightened of you. Scooters on the pavement still really irritate me, even with that knowledge!

Jamie (*laughs*) And lastly, we talked about addiction, which is such a mammoth topic. I was particularly fascinated by your concept of 'para-addictions' and how these affect us in our daily lives. It's interesting to see that we have strong urges to behave in ways that are *somewhat* harmful. And I liked the idea that we might have to be our own psychologist and figure out what kind of changes we need – and are willing – to make.

Robert Yes, and to try to make them, to evaluate what works and what doesn't, and then to try again.

Jamie The key point I took away is that although there are many paths into addiction, there are also many paths *out* of addiction. That seems to me very heartening.

Robert Learning about these principles can open up a lot of options and make things seem more possible.

Jamie It's been quite the eye-opener working on this book. And I can honestly say that putting some of these principles into practice has certainly enhanced my life. I do find myself engaging far more in rewarding and enjoyable cycles than in rewarding but un-enjoyable cycles! It's like riding a bike where the wheels turn smoothly.

Robert I'm very glad to hear it. As always, it's been a pleasure. And I look forward to our next book, *Reflect: The Science Of Decision Making*, where we'll be exploring the human brain and how we can harness it to make better decisions.

Jamie I can't wait! In the meantime, I'm going to order another garlic bread. I think I need one . . .

Glossary

Adaptation: A process in which we get used to something and come to expect it so that we are disappointed if our experience falls short or pleasantly surprised if it is exceeded.

Addiction: A tendency to experience powerful urges or desires to take drugs or engage in certain harmful behaviours, to such an extent that it can be regarded as a clinical condition that could benefit from treatment.

Animal Brain: In this book, it refers to the parts of our brain involved in sensation, perception, muscle control, emotions, habits, drives, and feelings of desire – all things that we share in some form or another with other animals.

Associative Learning: A form of learning in which an impulse to act, a feeling, or an idea, comes to be triggered by a stimulus that has often immediately preceded it. It includes habit learning, and Pavlovian (classical) conditioning. For example, learning to associates smells with pleasant experiences.

Behaviour: Physical actions involving our voluntary muscles, co-ordinated by our central nervous system.

Behaviour Repertoire: Behaviours that we have enacted before and are ready to enact when the opportunity arises.

Behavioural Substitution: A way of stopping ourselves doing something by finding something else to do that will serve at least some of the same purpose. For example, vaping instead of smoking.

COM-B Model: Capability, Opportunity, Motivation, and Behaviour. For any behaviour to occur, the person must have the capability, opportunity, and motivation to do it. The components of the model interact with each other.

Dopamine: A chemical that acts as a chemical messenger between nerve cells in the brain. Dopamine release by nerve terminals in the shell of the nucleus accumbens teaches the brain to repeat an action that has just been performed because it was pleasurable; dopamine release in the core of the nucleus accumbens teaches the brain to repeat an action that has just been performed purely on impulse.

Drive States: Feelings that arise from processes aimed at keeping us alive and producing offspring, such as hunger, thirst and sex drive.

Feelings: Parts of our subjective experience including emotions, drive states, urges, and sensations such as pain and nausea.

Fixed-ratio Schedule Of Reinforcement: Rewarding or punishing a behaviour after a fixed number of times a subject does it – for example, after exactly five occurrences.

Habit: A mental process in which an impulse to act stems directly from a stimulus as a result of associative learning. For example, shifting weight to maintain balance on a bicycle. (Note the difference from instinct which is innate.)

Habituation: A process in which a stimulus has less and less of an effect the more we are exposed to it. For example, getting used to a high-definition television. (Note: it has nothing to do with habits.)

Homeostatic Process: A process that works to keep some feature within limits – for example, blood glucose concentration.

Human Brain: In this book, it refers to the parts of our brain involved in reflective thought, planning and language.

Identity: Thoughts, feelings, and images about ourselves as we have been, as we are, and as we could be. It includes the groups we identify with and personal rules, such as 'I don't eat meat'.

IF-THEN Rule: A conscious plan to perform a very specific action in a very specific set of circumstances. Forming good IF-THEN rules is an important way of ensuring that we continue to enact personal rules. For example, IF someone offers me a cigarette at a party THEN I will always say, 'No thanks, I've quit'.

Impulse: The pattern of brain activity that is ultimately responsible for a given behaviour. Most of the time, it operates outside our awareness but is experienced as an 'urge' when we try to stop ourselves or are blocked by some outside force.

Inhibition: The pattern of brain activity that opposes an impulse. When it comes from a decision not to do something, it requires mental effort.

Instinct: A mental process in which an impulse to act stems directly from a stimulus without the need for any learning. For example, laughing when tickled.

Motivation: All the brain processes that energise and direct behaviour, including plans, evaluations, desires, habits, and instincts.

Need (subjective): A feeling of attraction to an imagined future scenario associated with anticipation of relief from, or avoidance of, mental or physical discomfort. For example, needing to scratch an itch.

Negative Reinforcer: A stimulus that, when it follows a particular action, weakens the impulse to perform that action in the future – also known as a punishment. It also strengthens the impulse to perform an action that stops or prevents it.

Non-reward: Not rewarding a behaviour that had previously been rewarded.

Nucleus Accumbens: A part of the brain near the hypothalamus that is central to motivation. Somewhat simplified: the outer part (the shell) underpins motivation to do something because we expect to enjoy it. The inner part (the core) underpins motivation to do things by impulse.

Operant Conditioning: An associative learning process in which an impulse to perform an action is increased or decreased as a result of what happens after that action – commonly thought of as learning by reward and punishment, but not requiring conscious decision making.

Overlearning: A process in which extensive repetition causes very strong associative learning.

Para-addiction: A tendency to experience strong urges or desires to repeatedly behave in certain ways that may be harmful to some extent.

Positive Reinforcer: A stimulus that, when it follows a particular action, strengthens the impulse to perform that action in the future – also known as a reward.

Primary Reinforcer: A stimulus that, when it follows a particular action, strengthens or weakens the impulse to perform that action in the future, and does so without the need for any learning. For example, tasty food for a hungry person.

Punish: Causing something negative to happen to someone because of something they have, or have not, done.

Ratio-strain: A tendency to stop responding when a task demands too many actions before any reward is attained. For example, struggling to complete a long project, such as a PhD thesis.

Reward (noun): A more user-friendly name for a positive reinforcer, though somewhat misleading because it is taken to imply that the stimulus is enjoyable when it doesn't have to be.

Reward (verb): Providing a stimulus that acts as a reward. For example, paying someone for doing a job.

Satiation: A process in which a drive state is reduced and sometimes eventually reversed. For example, eating a large meal can reduce or eliminate hunger and then eating can even become aversive.

Secondary Reinforcer: A stimulus that comes to act as a positive or negative reinforcer as a result of being associated with a reward or punishment. For example, the feeling of smoke being drawn into the mouth and lungs comes to reinforce the act of smoking because it is immediately followed by a 'nicotine hit' which is rewarding

Sensitisation: A process in which a stimulus has a stronger and stronger effect the more we are exposed to it. For example, irritation caused by a dog barking at night.

Stimulus: Something that happens that sets off a response. It could be something in one's mind, such as a thought that triggers an emotion, or something in the world. For example, a memory of dinner last night may trigger a desire to eat leftovers, or opening the fridge and seeing the leftovers may trigger the same desire.

Successive Approximation: A way of training a behaviour in stages, rewarding actions that are closer and closer to the one desired.

Testosterone: A hormone produced mainly by the testes (in males) that causes the development of male sexual organs and physique as well as typically male behaviour patterns such as aggression and risk taking. A smaller amount is also produced by females.

Theory Of Evolution: The theory, now established beyond doubt, that members of a species evolve over successive generations by random mutations occurring in their genes, some of which increase the ability to survive and reproduce. Members with these genes become more common, and members of a species with less adaptive genes become less common. At some point, the divergence of a lineage within a species becomes so great that members can no longer breed successfully with other lineages, and a new species is formed.

Urge: The subjective experience of an impulse to perform a specific behaviour that is being frustrated because we are stopping ourselves or cannot do it immediately.

Variable-ratio Schedule Of Reinforcement: Rewarding or punishing a behaviour intermittently and unpredictably.

Want (subjective): A feeling of attraction to an imagined future scenario associated with anticipated pleasure or satisfaction. For example, wanting to eat a bar of chocolate.

Withdrawal Symptoms: Adverse symptoms that emerge when people cut down on or stop using a drug that their brain has adapted to. These are usually temporary, lasting from a few days to a few months.

Further Reading

West, R & West, J. *Energise: The Secrets of Motivation.* **London: Silverback, 2019.**
Energise is the first book in this series. It introduces key ideas about motivation, including what shapes it and how it drives our behaviour. It's written in the same conversational style as *React: Harness Your Animal Brain.*

West, R & Brown, J. *Theory of Addiction.* **Oxford: Wiley, 2013.**
This book reviews the major theories of addiction, which is a disorder of motivation. Thus, this book provides a handy review of theories of motivation. It also introduces the PRIME Theory of Motivation, which aims to bring all these theories together and is the academic foundation of this book series.

Weiner, B. *Human Motivation.* **Hove: Psychology Press, 2013.**
A classic text from one of the giants in the field of motivation. This book was originally published in 1980 but was republished in 2013. Although a very ambitious text, it does not seek to provide a fully integrated account.

Mook, D. *Motivation: The Organization of Action.* **New York: WW Norton, 1987.**
This superb book is a tour de force that covers all the main theories of motivation. However, like Weiner's *Human Motivation,* it does not attempt to integrate them.

Acknowledgements

As always, we are deeply indebted to Aliyah Keshani for editing this series. Thanks also go to Matthew West for his excellent illustrations and design. We would also like to extend our appreciation to the students of University College London's Summer Schools and MSc in Behaviour Change for their invaluable comments on the draft versions of the text.

React: Harness Your Animal Brain is part of a series of short volumes about behaviour change, called 'Unlocking Behaviour Change'. The idea behind the series is that influencing behaviour is like getting the code for a combination lock. Everything needs to be in place in terms of the person's capability, opportunity and motivation to engage in the behaviour. The series is published in association with University College London's *Centre for Behaviour Change* to which a share of the royalties go to support its work.

About The Authors

Robert West is Professor Emeritus of Health Psychology at University College London (UCL) and an Associate of UCL's *Centre for Behaviour Change*. He is a former Editor-in-Chief of the specialist scientific journal *Addiction*, and he has published more than 900 scholarly works, including books on behaviour change, addiction, and smoking.

Jamie West is a writer, performer and musician. He holds a BA in English from UCL and an MA in Creative Writing from Birkbeck University. For more information, visit: www.jamiewest.net.

Illustrations and design: Matthew West

Image concepts: Jamie West, Aliyah Keshani, Matthew West and Robert West

Printed in Great Britain
by Amazon

85364123R00108